Guideposts

FOR THE

Spirit

STORIES OF

Friendship

Guideposts

FOR THE

Spirit

STORIES OF

Friendship

GuidepostsBooks®
New York, New York

Guideposts for the Spirit: Stories of Friendship

ISBN-13: 978-0-8249-4721-7
ISBN-10: 0-8249-4721-5

Published by GuidepostsBooks
16 East 34th Street
New York, New York 10016
www.guidepostsbooks.com

Distributed by Ideals Publications, a Guideposts company
535 Metroplex Drive, Suite 250
Nashville, Tennessee 37211

GuidepostsBooks and *Ideals* are registered trademarks of Guideposts, Carmel, New York.

Edited by Julie K. Hogan
Cover art: "Dance of the Sunflowers" © 2001 by Camille Engel, www.camille-engel.com
Cover designed by Marisa Jackson
Interior designed by Royce DeGrie

Library of Congress CIP data is on file.

Printed and bound in Italy by LEGO

10 9 8 7 6 5 4 3 2 1

CONTENTS

The Meaning of Friendship

Friends are the sunshine of life.
—JOHN HAY

ON FRIENDSHIP

KAHLIL GIBRAN

*Y*our friend is your needs answered. He is your field which you sow with love and reap with thanksgiving. And he is your board and your fireside. For you come to him with your hunger, and you seek him for peace.

When your friend speaks his mind, you fear not the "nay" in your own mind nor do you withhold the "ay." And when he is silent your heart ceases not to listen to his heart; for without words, in friendship, all thoughts, all desires, all expectations are born and shared with joy that is unacclaimed. When you part from your friend, you grieve not; for that which you love most in him may be clearer in his absence, as the mountain to the climber is clearer from the plain.

And let there be no purpose in friendship save the deepening of the spirit. For love that seeks aught but the disclosure of its own mystery is not love, but a net cast forth and only the unprofitable is caught.

And let your best be for your friend. If he must know the ebb of your tide, let him know its flood also. For what is your friend that you should seek him with hours to kill? Seek him always with hours to live. For it is his to fill your need but not your emptiness. And in the sweetness of friendship let there be laughter and sharing of pleasures.

For in the dew of little things the heart finds its morning and is refreshed.

What is a friend? A single soul dwelling in two bodies.
—ARISTOTLE

A COMMON QUEST
C. S. LEWIS

The common quest or vision which unites friends does not absorb them in such a way that they remain ignorant or oblivious of one another. On the contrary, it is the very medium in which their mutual love and knowledge exist. One knows nobody so well as one's "fellow." Every step of the common journey tests his mettle; and the tests are tests we fully understand because we are undergoing them ourselves. Hence, as he rings true time after time, our reliance, our respect, and our admiration blossom into an appreciative love of a singularly robust and well-informed kind. If, at the outset, we had attended more to him and less to the thing our friendship is "about," we should not have come to know or love him so well. You will not find the warrior, the poet, the philosopher, or the Christian by staring in his eyes as if he were your mistress; better fight beside him, read with him, argue with him, pray with him.

—

Friendship is something that raised us almost above humanity. This love, free from instinct, free from all duties but those which love has freely assumed, almost wholly free from jealousy, and free without qualification from the need to be needed, is eminently spiritual. It is the sort of love one can imagine between angels.

If there is any one secret of success,
it lies in the ability to get the other person's point of view
and see things from his angle as well as your own.
—HENRY FORD

FROM NOTES ON ENGLISH CHARACTER

E. M. FORSTER

*O*nce upon a time (this is an anecdote), I went for a week's holiday on the Continent with an Indian friend. We both enjoyed ourselves and were sorry when the week was over; but on parting, our behaviour was absolutely different. He was plunged in despair. He felt that because the holiday was over, all happiness was over until the world ended. He could not express his sorrow too much. But in me the Englishman came out strong. I reflected that we should meet again in a month or two and could write in the interval if we had anything to say; and under these circumstances I could not see what there was to make a fuss about. It wasn't as if we were parting forever or dying. "Buck up," I said, "do buck up." He refused to buck up, and I left him plunged in gloom.

The conclusion of the anecdote is even more instructive. For when we met the next month, our conversation threw a good deal of light on the English character. I began by scolding my friend. I told him that he had been wrong to feel and display so much emotion upon so slight an occasion, that it was inappropriate. The word "inappropriate" roused him to fury. "What?" he cried. "Do you measure out your emotions as if they were potatoes?" I did not like the simile of the potatoes, but after a moment's reflection I said, "Yes, I do; and what's

4

more, I think I ought to. A small occasion demands a little emotion, just as a large occasion demands a great one. I would like my emotions to be appropriate. This may be measuring them like potatoes, but it is better than slopping them about like water from a pail, which is what you did." He did not like the simile of the pail. "If those are your opinions, they part us forever," he cried and left the room. Returning immediately, he added: "No, but your whole attitude toward emotion is wrong. Emotion has nothing to do with appropriateness. It matters only that it shall be sincere. I happened to feel deeply. I showed it. It doesn't matter whether I ought to have felt deeply or not."

This remark impressed me very much. Yet I could not agree with it and said that I valued emotion as much as he did but used it differently; if I poured it out on small occasions, I was afraid of having none left for the great ones and of being bankrupt at the crises of life. Note the word "bankrupt." I spoke as a member of a prudent, middle-class nation, always anxious to meet my liabilities. But my friend spoke as an Oriental, and the Oriental has behind him a tradition, not of middle-class prudence, but of kingly munificence and splendour. He feels his resources are endless, just as John Bull feels his are finite. As regards material resources, the Oriental is clearly unwise. Money isn't endless. If we spend or give away all the money we have, we haven't any more and must take the consequences, which are frequently unpleasant. But as regards the resources of the spirit, he may be right. The emotions may be endless. The more we express them, the more we may have to express.

The fingers of God touch your life when you touch a friend.
—MARY DAWN HUGHES

THE HANDSHAKE

BEN PURCELL

At the first stab of dawn a rooster crowed. For a moment—a cruelly brief moment—I was back at the family farm in Clarkesville, Georgia, my wife, Anne, slumbering beside me, our five children snug in their beds down the hall. I could almost feel Anne's sturdy warmth. But as the sun pierced the tiny, barred window and forced open my eyes, I was jerked back to my true surroundings: a North Vietnamese POW camp, "home" for the three years since I'd been captured during the bloody Tet offensive in February 1968.

I eased into a sitting position on the wooden slab that was my bunk, trying to stretch out the ache in my back. My eye roamed the dingy cell. I knew every inch of it. It was all I knew. Three years of total isolation.

I received no word from home, no contact with other prisoners. I'd not even been allowed to write Anne, though in my heart I spoke to her day and night, praying God would keep her and the children safe and let them know I was surviving.

Survival. I had to keep my mind disciplined. In my thoughts I "reread" the books from my college literature classes: *Oliver Twist, Crime and Punishment, Of Human Bondage.* One guard reminded me a bit of Henry Fonda, and that got me projecting my favorite movies on a bright, wide internal screen. I watched *My Darling Clementine* again and again, slowing down and replaying favorite scenes.

And I never strayed from my greatest comfort. Daily I read Scripture—not that I was actually permitted a Bible. But deep in my mind I read and reread it until the pages were smudged, creased, and tattered.

Still there were moments I thought I might snap. Worse than any torture, the sheer agony of solitude, of being unable to experience the simplest human contact, was what I feared would finally undo me. Somehow I think my captors knew that too.

God, I prayed that morning as I did every morning, please help ease the loneliness. *Give me strength to go on.*

Slipping off my bunk I began my daily routine. I was required to sweep out my cell. I relished the job. It brought order and purpose to the start of my day. As usual, I took my broom and went over every precious foot of floor. When I finished I flicked the small pile of sweepings through a four-inch gap at the bottom of my door into the passageway beyond, where some unseen camp trusty would sweep it up for collection.

Suddenly the little pile was swept briskly back into my cell.

Odd, I thought. *Why would he do that?*

I pushed the pile back out, thinking the trusty had made a mistake. It came right back in. *This is deliberate,* I realized testily.

I swept it out. Again it came back.

Now I was mad. I flicked the trash back under the door and got down on my hands and knees. As soon as the broom came toward the gap again, I reached under and grabbed it.

"Không!" the trusty hissed, Vietnamese for no. He jerked back the broom but I held on, terrier-tight. For a moment we grunted and tussled. His struggling told me he was frightened. If he was caught messing with one of the American POWs, he'd be harshly dealt with.

I thought about that. He was, after all, a prisoner, like me. Why get him into any more trouble than what had already landed him here? So I turned the broom loose. *That'll teach him a lesson, though,* I told myself.

It was curious that I didn't hear him scuffling off. I'd have thought he would have wanted to get away from the crazy American. Instead there was just his labored breathing on the other side of the door. I stayed on my knees by the opening, straining for some clue to his behavior. Finally he was silent. I wasn't even sure he was still there when, to my astonishment, the strangest thing happened: he thrust his thin hand under my cell door. I stepped back. He slapped his palm on the floor, then offered it to me in the form of a handshake.

I froze. Maybe this was a trick. But something silently whispered reassurance that the man on the other side was trying to reach out to me.

Slowly I stretched my fingers toward his, almost afraid to touch another human being again in friendship. When I lightly felt his hand he quickly pulled my fingers into his hungry grip. A kind of warm physical music played throughout me, a combustion of feelings that had been trapped for so long. I put my other hand over his, covering our grip. Then he reached under the door and did the same.

It was a dangerous moment; we let it linger as long as we could. Then quickly we both withdrew our hands.

I never encountered that trusty again, whoever he was—a North Vietnamese civilian, a South Vietnamese soldier? But for a moment we were just two human beings reaching out. In the remaining two years of my captivity, I was sustained by the simple touch of a hand. It was that one moment of caring human contact that I so desperately needed, that we all need, to go on.

A true friend is the gift of God,
and He only who made hearts can unite them.
—Robert South

Thoughts on Friendship

Ralph Waldo Emerson

I awoke this morning with devout thanksgiving for my friends, the old and the new. Shall I not call God the Beautiful, who daily showeth Himself so to me in His gifts? I chide society, I embrace solitude, and yet I am not so ungrateful as not to see the wise, the lovely, and the noble-minded, as from time to time they pass my gate. Who hears me, who understands me, becomes mine—a possession for all time. Nor is Nature so poor but she gives me this joy several times, and thus we weave social threads of our own, a new web of relations; and, as many thoughts in succession substantiate themselves, we shall by and by stand in a new world of our own creation, and no longer strangers and pilgrims in a traditionary globe. My friends have come to me unsought. The great God gave them to me. By oldest right, by the divine affinity of virtue with itself, I find them, or rather not I, but the Deity in me and in them derides and cancels the thick walls of individual character, relation, age, sex, circumstance, at which he usually connives, and now makes many one. High thanks I owe you, excellent lovers, who carry out the world for me to new and noble depths and enlarge the meaning of all my thoughts.

A cheer, then, for the noble breast
that fears not danger's post;
And like the lifeboat, proves a friend,
When friends are wanted most.
—ELIZA COOK

CONCERNING FRIENDSHIP

HARRY B. HAWES

*A*ll that can be expected of any man is to make the best use of the things that are within his power. Only the contented man is rich, so we must look for the things that bring contentment. And first of these is to find a friend; and if you find two friends, you are indeed a lucky man; and if you find three friends, real friends, then you are a rich and powerful man.

In prosperity it is easy to find a friend, but in adversity it is most difficult of all things. No matter how small a man's means may be, if he gives of what he has to his friend, it is the same as if it were a great amount.

A man's pleasures are ensured by sharing them with a friend, and his griefs are reduced by securing the sympathy of a friend.

The counsel of a friend is the best counsel because it will be true advice; for when received from a mere acquaintance, it may be so filled with flattery that its value will be destroyed; and faithful and true counsel rarely comes excepting from the true friend.

It is said that in youth we have visions and in old age, dreams, and the vision and the dream may give us an ideal of perfection; but experience and large contact with men compel us to accept the man who measures in his virtues only the substantial average.

If we view a man as a whole and find him good as a friend, we must not be diverted from the happy average—the everyday, human average—by using a magnifying glass upon his faults or frailties. We must, in order to have and hold a friend, accept him as he is, demanding but one thing in return for our affection—his fidelity.

God gives us friends to bless the present scene.
—EDWARD YOUNG

THE TAMALE-MAKER'S GIFT OF FRIENDSHIP

BETSY RAMELKAMP

*I*s it time to get the tamales, Mama?" I spoke softly for fear of awakening my little brother, who was napping in the next room.

"Almost, honey." She looked up from folding a stack of fresh laundry on the kitchen table. "When Jean gets home from school and can look after Eddie, then we'll go."

I was a kindergartner living in West Los Angeles near a neighborhood named Sawtelle when I first became acquainted with the Mexican delicacy the *tamal*. In the United States, we call it the tamale. At the time, this was not a familiar food for our family. My Southern mother was well-schooled in the art of Kentucky cooking but not in Cal-Mex. However, once a neighbor introduced us to these hot, freshly made concoctions and told us they could be purchased for ten cents apiece in a house just a mile away, we became aficionados.

Sawtelle was a mixed Anglo-Hispanic-Oriental community, which had once been a separate town before Los Angeles swallowed it up. It lay a few miles east of the Pacific Ocean.

Mrs. Ochoa lived in an old frame house on a narrow, tree-lined street. Every Friday we drove over to buy our family's end-of-the-week treat. It was more than just an errand to me, however. It was an adventure, a glimpse into another life, redolent with spicy smells, where people's conversations were sprinkled with words I didn't understand. The radio blared rollicking band music and on the walls were pictures of saints and martyrs.

We walked up shallow, sagging steps and banged on the screen door, calling out, "Mrs. Ochoa!" a name that sounded like a sneeze to me.

Sometimes the tamale-maker herself appeared, but more often it was her oldest daughter, Elena, who answered our shouts. All four of the Ochoa girls helped their mother in the making and selling of tamales.

Olive-skinned, with softly waving black hair and limpid dark eyes, they ranged in ages from fourteen to twenty years. Also, a group of small, noisy boys played on the living room floor or in the front yard.

"*Hola!* Come in." Although the Ochoas were an old California family and spoke English well, their speech was peppered with Spanish expressions.

"Mama's outside cooking the tamales." She led us through the house and out the kitchen door into the tree-shaded backyard.

Looking at Mrs. Ochoa, one could understand why all the children were pretty. She was short and plump with dimpled cheeks and elbows, rosy brown skin, and merry dark eyes. Her black hair was pulled back into a loose bun, with curly tendrils plastered about her face and neck due to the moisture coming from two steaming tubs.

These were really washtubs of galvanized metal that sat on top of bricks and had chicken-wire racks to hold the food over boiling water. Wood fires, burning down to coals, fueled the makeshift cookers. On top of the racks lay dozens of small, cornhusk-wrapped packets.

I knew that inside those protective coverings were rolls of firm, rich, cornmeal mush, filled with spicy shredded meat, olives, and chili sauce. These would be the main dish in our meal that night. Mrs. Ochoa was leaning over one of the tubs and turning the packets when we appeared.

"Ah, Señora! And the little señorita." She smiled down at me. "Will it be the usual this afternoon?"

"Yes, six of the usual," replied Mama. "They're so delicious, I daren't change the menu or my family will fuss."

Mrs. Ochoa took six hot tamales from the nearest tub and began to wrap them in newspapers stacked on a workbench. She gestured toward the other tub. "One day you must try our sweet tamales. They are filled with my own guava jam and are *deliciosos*."

"I'll fix Spanish rice to go with the 'hot' ones, and that will be plenty for my family," said Mama firmly. "Six of the regular, thank you."

Young as I was, I knew that Mama was short of money and couldn't afford to buy more than six tamales.

Over the years, we became quite friendly with the Ochoas.

I loved going to their house, chatting with the girls and joking with the playful little boys.

I even learned a few words of Spanish. I loved the color, noise, constant activity, and always, the delectable aromas. My mother, too, struck up a real friendship with Mrs. Ochoa.

"They're lovely people," Mama said to my father one night. "It's good for Bets to go over there. She learns a lot from them. Mrs. Ochoa is a fine woman with nice manners." That clinched it as far as she was concerned.

One Friday we went over as usual. After wrapping our six

"hot ones," Mrs. Ochoa laid another sheet of newspaper on her workbench. On it, to our surprise, she began to place six more, from the tub of sweet tamales.

"Just the usual six, please," Mama said quickly.

"Oh, but these are a *regalo*—a gift, Señora. For the little girl. Is not her birthday today?"

"How in the world did you know that?"

"She mention to my Elena."

Mama glanced down at me with stern surprise. "Why, Betsy!"

"She asked me, Mama! Last Friday."

"But six extra tamales, Mrs. Ochoa! I'm afraid we can't accept . . ."

"Please. You accept. Is nice to try something different." She handed me the extra package. "And is nice, sometimes, to give gifts. Happy birthday, little miss!"

The following Friday we returned, as usual. We praised the delicious sweet tamales, which had added an extra fillip to my birthday dinner.

Then we purchased our usual six hot ones. Just before we left, my mother sent me back to our car.

"We have something for you, Mrs. Ochoa."

I carried the carefully wrapped box into the living room and handed it up to our friend. Opening it, she gasped at the sight of a large cake glazed with caramel and decorated with walnuts.

"It's my Kentucky Nut Cake." Mama was smiling. "As you said, it's nice to give gifts."

The language of friendship is not words, but meanings.
—HENRY DAVID THOREAU

FROM A WEEK ON THE CONCORD AND MERRIMACK RIVERS

HENRY DAVID THOREAU

*N*o word is oftener on the lips of men than friendship, and indeed no thought is more familiar to their aspirations. All men are dreaming of it, and its drama, which is always a tragedy, is enacted daily. It is the secret of the universe. You may thread the town, you may wander the country, and none shall ever speak of it, yet thought is everywhere busy about it, and the idea of what is possible in this respect affects our behavior toward all new men and women, and a great many old ones. . . .

Of what use the friendliest dispositions even, if there are no hours given to friendship, if it is forever postponed to unimportant duties and relations? Friendship is first, friendship last. But it is equally impossible to forget our friends, and to make them answer to our ideal. When they say farewell, then indeed we begin to keep them company. How often we find ourselves turning our backs on our actual friends, that we may go and meet their ideal cousins. I would that I were worthy to be any man's friend.

—

The language of friendship is not words, but meanings. It is an intelligence above language. One imagines endless conversations with his friend in which the tongue shall be loosed and thoughts be spoken without hesitancy or end; but the experience is commonly far otherwise. Acquaintances may come and go and have a word ready for every occasion; but what puny word shall he utter whose very breath is thought and meaning? . . .

But all that can be said of friendship is like botany to flowers. How can the understanding take account of its friendliness?

Real friendship is shown in times of trouble.
—EURIPIDES

A CONSTANT FRIEND

LAURA INGALLS WILDER, JANUARY 1917

A group of friends was gathered around a glowing fire the other evening. The cold outside and the warmth and cheer and soft lights within had opened their hearts, and they were talking freely together as good friends should.

"I propose that we eliminate the word 'can't' from our vocabularies for the coming year," said Mrs. Betty. "There ain't no such animal anyhow."

"But sometimes we just c–t" began sister Sue, then stopped abruptly at the sound of an amused chuckle.

"Oh, well, if you feel that way about it!" rejoined Mrs. Betty. "But I still insist that if you see such an animal, it is only a creature of the imagination. When I went to school they tried to teach me that it was noble to say 'I'll try' when confronted with a difficult thing to be done, but it always sounded weak to me. Why, the very expression presupposes failure!" She went on with growing earnestness. "Why not say 'I will' and then make good? One can, you know, for if there is not one way to do a thing, there are usually two."

"That word 'can't' with its suggestion of failure!" exclaimed George. "Do you know a man came up to me on the street the other day and said, 'You can't lend me a dollar, can you?' He expected to fail in his request—and he most certainly did."

"After all," said brother James slowly, "people do a good deal as they are expected to do, even to saying the things they are expected to say. The power of suggestion is very strong. Did you ever notice how everyone will agree with you on the weather? I have tried it out many a time just for fun. Before the days of motor cars, when we could speak as we passed driving along the road, I have said to the first man I met, 'This is a fine day'; and regardless of what the weather might be, he never would fail to answer, 'Sure, it's a fine day' or something to that effect and pass on smiling. To the next man I met I would say, 'Cold weather we're having,' and his reply would always be, 'Coldest I ever knew at this season,' or 'Mighty cold this morning,' and he would go on his way shivering.

"No matter if it's raining, a man usually will agree with you that it's awfully dry weather if you suggest it to him right."

"Speaking of friends," said Philip, which no one had been doing, though all could trace the connecting thought. "Speaking of friends—I heard a man say not long ago that he could count all the friends he had on the fingers of one hand. I wonder . . ." and his voice trailed off into silence as his thought carried him away. A chorus of protest arose.

"Oh, how awful!" exclaimed Pansy, with tender eyes. "Anyone has more friends than that. Why, if anybody is sick or in trouble, everybody is his friend."

"It all depends on one's definition of friend," said Mrs. Betty in a considering tone. "What do we mean when we say 'friend'? What is the test for a friend?" A silence fell upon the little group around the glowing fire.

"But I want to know," insisted Mrs. Betty. "What is the test for a friend? Just what do you mean, Philip, when you say, 'He is my friend'?"

"Well," Philip replied, "when a man is my friend I expect he will stand by me in trouble, that he will do whatever he can to help me if I am needing help, and do it at once even at cost of inconvenience to himself."

"Now, Pansy! How do you know your friends?" still insisted Mrs. Betty.

"My friends," said Pansy, with the tender eyes, "will like me anyway, no matter what my faults are. They will let me do as I please and not try to change me but will be my friends whatever I do."

"Next," began Mrs. Betty, but there were exclamations from every side. "No! No! It's your turn now! We want to know what your test of friendship is!"

"Why! I was just asking for information," answered Mrs. Betty with a brilliant smile, the warmth of which included the whole circle. "I wanted to know—"

"Tell us! Tell us!" they all insisted.

"Well, then," earnestly, "my friends will stand by me in trouble. They will love me even though I make mistakes and in spite of my faults, but if they see me in danger of taking the wrong course, they will warn me. If necessary they will even tell me of a fault which perhaps is growing on me unaware. One should dare anything for a friend, you know."

"Yes, but to tell friends of a fault is dangerous," said gentle Rosemary. "It is so likely to make them angry."

"To be sure," Mrs. Betty answered. "But if we are a friend, we will take it thankfully for the sake of the spirit in which it is given as we do a Christmas present which otherwise we would not care for."

Remember well and bear in mind,
A constant friend is hard to find,
And when you find one good and true,
Change not the old one for the new,

quoted Philip as the group began to break up.

"No, don't change 'em," said George, in the bustle of putting on of wraps. "Don't change 'em! Just take 'em all in!"

There is only one thing better than making a new friend,
and that is keeping an old one.
—ELMER G. LETERMAN

A FRIEND IN DEED

DAWN VANDERLOO

*M*y father became friends with Virgil Zacharias at work. Their friendship grew on fishing trips and picnics with their young families. Their friendship strengthened after Virgil contracted polio and through the years that followed.

Virgil's sons became top high school athletes. Unfortunately, he had never been able to toss them a football or teach them how to make a lay-up. And, restricted to life in an iron lung, he would never be able to see them play.

Because of his friendship with Virgil, my father approached the phone company and persuaded them to install a telephone on the football field with a direct line into Virgil's home. From the sidelines my father reported every game, allowing Virgil to experience his sons' great plays. That winter, my father broadcast basketball games from the high school gym.

My father provided coverage for several seasons. I can still see him running back and forth along the football field or sitting atop the high school stage reporting each basketball play. The years passed and both Zacharias boys graduated. But until the day Virgil died, he never lost the memory of the games his sons played. And I'll never forget how my father taught me what it means to be a good friend.

A true friend unbosoms freely, advises justly, assists readily,
adventures boldly, takes all patiently, defends courageously,
and continues a friend unchangeably.
—William Penn

How to Treat a Friend

Jeremy Taylor

Give thy friend counsel wisely and charitably, but leave him to his liberty whether he will follow thee or no, and be not angry if thy counsel be rejected; for "advice is no empire," and he is not my friend that will be my judge whether I will or no. He that gives advice to his friend and exacts obedience to it does not the kindness and ingenuity of a friend but the office and pertness of a schoolmaster.

When you admonish your friend, let it be without bitterness; when you chide him, let it be without reproach; when you praise him, let it be with worthy purposes and for just causes and in friendly measures; too much of that is flattery, too little is envy; if you do it justly, you teach him true measures. But when others praise him, rejoice, though they praise not thee, and remember that if thou esteemest his praise to be thy disparagement, thou art envious but neither just nor kind.

After all this, treat thy friend nobly, love to be with him, do to him all the worthinesses of love and fair endearment, according to thy capacity and his; bear with his infirmities till they approach towards being criminal; but never dissemble with him, never despise him, never leave him.

No one is a friend to his friend who does not love in return.
—PLATO

THE LOVE UNDERLYING FRIENDSHIP

ERICH FROMM

The most fundamental kind of love, which underlies all types of love, is brotherly love. By this I mean the sense of responsibility, care, respect, knowledge of any other human being, the wish to further his life. This is the kind of love the Bible speaks of when it says love thy neighbor as thyself. Brotherly love is love for all human beings; it is characterized by its very lack of exclusiveness. If I have developed the capacity for love, then I cannot help loving my brothers. In brotherly love there is the experience of union with all men, of human solidarity, of human atonement. Brotherly love is based on the experience that we are all one. The differences in talents, intelligence, knowledge are negligible in comparison with the identity of the human core common to all men. In order to experience this identity, it is necessary to penetrate from the periphery to the core. If I perceive in another person mainly the surface, I perceive mainly the differences—that which separates us. If I penetrate to the core, I perceive our identity, the fact of our brotherhood. . . .

Yet, love of the helpless one, love of the poor and the stranger are the beginnings of brotherly love. To love one's flesh and blood is no achievement. The animal loves its young and cares for them. The helpless one loves his master, since his life depends on him; the child loves his parents, since he needs them. Only in the love of those who do not serve a purpose, love begins to unfold.

*Only friends will tell you the truths you need
to hear to make . . . your life bearable.*
—FRANCINE DU PLESSIX GRAY

FAITHFUL FRIENDS

PAMELA KENNEDY

I pulled the bundle of mail from the mailbox with anticipation, wondering what surprises were hidden in it today. Perhaps I would win a million dollars, receive a letter from family, or find a party invitation along with the inevitable bills and catalogues.

A small, blue envelope slipped from the stack and fluttered to the ground. Picking it up, I recognized the return address of a dear friend with whom I had enjoyed lunch earlier in the week. Once inside, I settled at the kitchen table to read the note. She cheerfully recalled our terrific lunch and conversation, but then her tone changed to one of concern as she reminded me of the time we had spent discussing a mutual acquaintance— gossiping, really. She closed the note with this statement: *"After thinking about what I said to you, I feel I should apologize to you and Maryanne. I wasn't a very good friend to either of you."*

Her remark startled me. It made me think about what it means to be a faithful friend. Most would agree that being a friend implies being loyal when we are face to face as well as when our backs our turned. But my friend had grasped a deeper truth: faithful friendship also means holding one another accountable when we sense danger on the horizon of our relationship. How easy it is today to isolate ourselves from one another, to avoid confrontation, to keep our friendships on a superficial level, and thus to deprive each other of opportunities for growth and maturity. It was not easy for my friend to declare her feelings of failure to me, but she risked that in order to deepen the honesty of our relationship. What I appreciated as much, however, was the gentle reminder that I, too, had wandered into the dangerous trap of gossip.

In the book of Proverbs, King Solomon writes, *"Faithful are the wounds of a friend; but the kisses of an enemy are deceitful."* When friends are truly faithful, they tell us not only what we want to hear, but also what we need to hear. This friendly honesty strengthens and encourages healthy, growing relationships.

Smiles Begin Friendships

*A word, a smile, and the stranger at your elbow
may become an interesting friend.*
—D. C. PEATTIE

GRANDMA AND THE PAPER GIRL

ELLA DUQUETTE

I squinted against the afternoon sunshine, looking out the window for the paperboy. Ever since a stroke had weakened my legs, I hadn't been able to get around so well. I depended on the paper to keep me up to date with a world from which I often felt disconnected. Finally I saw someone coming down the street. A girl, no more than ten or eleven years old, hurled a rolled-up newspaper toward my screen door. It landed with a thud.

"Just a minute," I called out the window. "Where's the usual carrier?"

"I'm the carrier now, lady," she said, hands on her hips.

"Well, the old one used to bring the paper in to me."

"Oh, yeah? Well, I can do that." She came in and plopped the paper onto my lap, and I got a better look at her. Frayed shorts and a cropped top—and it wasn't even summer yet! She tossed back her shoulder-length red hair and blew a huge pink bubble.

"I hate bubble gum," I said.

"Tough beans," she said.

I gasped. This snippy little thing needed to be taught some manners.

"The children around here call me Mrs. Lee, after my late husband."

"Well, you can call me Kristin," she said with a sassy tilt of her head, then bounded down the steps.

28

Just what I need, I thought. Nothing was easy anymore. Simple tasks like dusting and doing laundry were an ordeal these days. And baking, which I used to love, was far too much trouble. My husband, Lee, and most of my friends had passed on. Lately I had found myself wondering why the Lord had left me behind. It was clear to me, anyway, that if young people today all acted like that smart-alecky paper girl, I had been too long in this world.

Kristin's attitude didn't much improve over the following weeks. But I had to admit she never missed a day or forgot to bring the paper inside to me. She even took to sharing some small talk when she stopped by. She came in from a wicked rainstorm once and pulled the paper out from under her coat.

"H— of a day, huh, Gram?" she said, handing me the paper.

I could feel the muscles in my jaw tense. "Do you talk like that just to shock me?" I asked. "And I'm not your grandmother."

"I just talk like all my friends."

"Not in this house, you don't," I shot back. "In my day you'd have had your mouth washed out with soap."

She laughed. "You'd have some fight on your hands if you tried it, Gram," she said.

I threw up my hands. *Why do I even bother with you?* I wondered.

But she started coming by after her paper route and other times as well, chitchatting happily about school, her friends. Each time she left, it was as if a radio had been turned off. One day a bundle of newspapers slipped from her hands onto the floor and she uttered a dirty word. Instantly she clapped a hand over her mouth and said, "Oops! Sorry, Gram."

Well, she's learned something, I thought, smiling secretly.

I dug out some of my old photographs and outfits, thinking she might like to see them. She never tired of my stories of growing up on a farm, how we raised our own food and washed our clothes by hand. *All this girl needs is some pushing,* I thought. Why else would she keep coming back when I was always fussing at her over her clothes or talk? *God, is that why you're keeping me around—for Kristin?*

She showed me her report card when I asked one afternoon.

"This is awful," I said.

"I do better than lots of kids," she snapped.

"You're not 'lots of kids.' Have a little pride in yourself."

"Oh, Gram, you make such a big deal out of things," she said. But I kept after her about her grades.

A short time later Kristin gave up her paper route and shifted her visits to after school. I didn't ask why she kept coming to see me because, although I wouldn't have been caught dead admitting it, her visits had become the highlight of my days.

Once she told me, giggling, about some of her friends who had been shoplifting.

"That's nothing to laugh about, young lady," I said. "It's stealing, plain and simple."

"Well, I didn't do it."

"All the same, you could be guilty by association. Your reputation goes with you all your life, you know."

"Oh, Gram, stop preaching."

"If you don't like it, there's the door," I declared. But she didn't leave. In fact, we spent more time together. Still, we had our moments. Like when she baked a cake, then sank down on a chair without laying a finger to the mound of dishes.

"Come back here and clean up after yourself," I ordered.

"No way. I'm not putting my hands in that sink. It's gross." She had just polished her nails—a ghastly purple.

"Tough beans!" I blurted. She laughed. *Mercy,* I thought. *Now I'm starting to talk like her.* But she did the dishes that day and many another. I taught her how to bake fresh bread and my famous apple pie. It was wonderful to smell those familiar smells coming from the kitchen again. One Sunday Kristin stopped by. "You didn't go to church dressed like that, did you?" I asked.

She glanced at her shorts and T-shirt. "All the kids dress like this."

"I've told you before, Kristin, you're not 'all the kids.'"

"Well, I suppose you think I should wear one of your old outfits, complete with hat and long white gloves!" She flounced out the door, only to come back a moment later. "I'm sorry, Gram," she said, giving me a quick hug. "Forgive me?"

How could I not? Making up with her seemed as natural as making up with one of my own daughters after a fight. Gradually, Kristin started dusting and cleaning up around the house, without the slightest hint from me. She even did my laundry. It chafed at my pride to let her do things I had done for myself all my life, but she was insistent. And this was the same girl who just a short while earlier wouldn't put her hands into a sink of dirty dishes!

"How about I set your hair?" she asked one day. "My mom taught me."

This was too much. "I'm not so old and helpless that I can't take care of myself."

"Oh, don't be so stubborn. Come on, Gram," she wheedled. For the first time that nickname didn't annoy me. I gave in, and she proceeded to work several different lathery formulas into my short locks, not letting me look in a mirror until she was done. I had visions of my hair dyed the same awful purple as her fingernails. I was amazed to find it soft, shiny, and still blond. "You're good at this," I said, and Kristin beamed.

I was even more impressed when, shortly after graduating from eighth grade, Kristin brought me a scrapbook filled with certificates of academic achievement.

"See, I told you that you weren't like everybody," I said, hugging her. "You're special." It was wonderful to see that she valued my approval. But the best part was seeing that she was pleased with herself.

I still didn't think much of her study habits. She insisted on keeping the television on when she did homework. I couldn't fathom how she could concentrate with that racket. But then there was a lot I couldn't fathom about Kristin's world. "Gram, do you know there are eight girls pregnant in the freshman class?" she told me. I gasped. "And that's nothing," she continued. "In some schools they have police guards and metal detectors and just about everybody smokes, drinks, and takes drugs."

I shuddered. *It's so different nowadays, Lord. How can I help her deal with all these things I know nothing about?* Then I thought of how far Kristin had already come, and I knew the best thing I could do was to keep being there for her, as she always was for me.

One evening recently she brought over a cake mix. "I'm going to bake us a super-duper double-chocolate cake, Gram," she announced.

"No way," I said. "Shortcuts won't make a cake as good as from scratch."

"Oh, come on, Gram. It's easier this way."

"Don't 'Oh, Gram' me, young lady. Easier isn't always better and in this house—" She broke into laughter—the laughter I had come to know so well—and in a moment, I joined in.

Kristin shook her head and took my hand. "I don't know what it is, Gram," she said. "We hardly ever agree on anything and you make me so mad sometimes. But I always come back. I guess I must love you."

Who would have known that when I looked out the window for the paper carrier that afternoon five years ago, I would end up finding my best friend?

A real friend is one who walks in
when the rest of the world walks out.
—WALTER WINCHELL

A CULTURE SHOCK

JOHN C. HAWLEY

When I graduated from high school, left the farm in Pennsylvania, and went off to college in New York, I thought living in the big city would be great and grown-up. Believing that God was leading me, I enrolled in the College of Insurance in Manhattan. But I was not prepared for the culture shock of urban life or the good dose of homesickness that hit.

Since most of the students at my college were commuters, the school did not have a dormitory. I found a room in Brooklyn Heights at the Hotel St. George, an old building occupied by many elderly residents. I could not have felt more out of place. Each time I crossed the lobby I came under the scrutiny of several older women who gave everyone the once-over.

Some days I had early afternoon classes, which other students loved, since they could beat the commuter rush. For me it meant heading back to my room for a long night of reading. I often felt so discouraged that I didn't know how to pray or what to ask for.

Then one afternoon after I had been back from classes for only a few minutes, someone knocked on the door. "Come in," I said. But no one entered, and the knock came again. So I opened the door.

Standing in the hall was a man I had seen most mornings on the street, always coming from the subway. I realized I hadn't seen him for the past few weeks.

"Hello, my name is Frank Hickey," he blurted out. Then he rattled on, "May I come in? I've had a nervous breakdown, and my psychiatrist says I need to make friends with you because you are my neighbor."

My mind raced. Was this safe? Was I getting myself into trouble? Mother had warned me to be careful of strangers. "Sure," I said. "Come in. Sit in the good chair."

As soon as he sat I told him my name, adding, "I'm a student at the College of Insurance." That was all I could manage, since I was unwilling to open up and not sure how smart it was to deal with this fellow.

"Well, I'm retired now," Frank said. "Used to work for the Customs Service, until a few months ago. I've had little to do since and haven't adjusted well. You are the only person who has talked to me for a while."

At first I was puzzled; then I remembered. I had always said "Good morning" or "Hello." In my small town those were the standard greetings when you saw someone on the street. But that was all I remembered saying, just "Good morning." Did that really count as conversation? My mind was filled with questions, but all I could ask was, "Where were you coming from when I saw you those mornings?"

"I go to early Mass over at St. John's," he said, "then catch the subway home and have breakfast. Always have the special. Always have the right change for the bill and a tip, so nobody has to speak to me. During the day I sit in my room, sometimes listening to the radio, sometimes just reading the papers."

Frank Hickey was slender, with olive skin; his horn-rimmed glasses and peppered hair gave him a distinguished appearance. He surely must have been an impressive customs officer. I had trouble believing this normal-looking person was having a serious problem, but then again, I probably didn't look homesick either.

"The doctor told me to make friends, talk to people whether I think I need to or not, and get into doing things," Frank went on. "He told me I could do anything except sit around and do nothing."

"What are you going to do first?"

"Already did it—came to see you."

Our chat was over in maybe five minutes, but from that day we talked regularly. As soon as Frank learned what I was studying, he scouted articles in the papers for me and read me the headlines in the evening while I drank coffee.

Frank taught me how to cope with the direct current in the building as well as how to deal with the heat. My room was so hot I had to leave a window open all winter. He showed me that I could stand milk and soda on the sill to keep them cool overnight. I told him of country ways.

He also explained why the old women always sat in the lobby: they kept track of who was up and about. If someone didn't follow a regular schedule, they put out the alarm. Since the hotel had many elderly residents in poor health, this was perhaps a way to save a life.

On holidays Frank usually visited his married sister, whose last name he never mentioned. Later he shared his dream of learning Italian and making a trip to Italy to see where his mother's forebears had lived.

Frank never asked me about the weekends I was away or about my occasional dates and family gatherings. But he did mention frequently that whenever he was invited to stay longer at his sister's, he didn't feel comfortable intruding into their lives.

I hated the confines of the nine-by-twelve rooms where we lived, but it didn't seem to bother Frank. His room had a second window, from which he could see the Brooklyn Bridge. That didn't include the sink and closet space, but still it didn't match the farmhouse I had grown up in.

After three years my college leased space for a dorm, and I was excited to move in with classmates. Frank seemed happy for me too. By then he had mastered enough Italian to make his trip, and his departure date was close to my moving date. We agreed we would move on and do new things without being sad or trying to keep in touch.

But some months after I had moved, I went back to the St. George and inquired about two things: Was Frank back yet, and could I buy some used furniture?

"No, Frank is not back and probably won't be," the desk clerk said. "The rooms where you lived were ruined when the steam pipe burst. The doors of your rooms were blown clear across the hall. All the furniture in your room and Frank's was ruined. If you had been there, you'd be dead.

"I think Frank has gone to visit his sister," the clerk added. "Can't give you the address."

I left and thought a lot about Frank Hickey. He wouldn't think of himself as an angel, but he sure seemed to be the answer to my unspoken prayer. For he helped one homesick kid get used to life in the big city.

*The most called-upon prerequisite
of a friend is an accessible ear.*
—MAYA ANGELOU

LOOK AGAIN

PAMELA KENNEDY

*H*elen was a woman everyone admired. She knew how to accomplish things. If you were in charge of something, you wanted Helen on your committee; and if she were the chairperson, she had no trouble recruiting volunteers.

She seemed to have a knack for making events successful as well as special. When she was in charge of the banquet, everyone remarked at the beautiful color scheme, the unique centerpieces, and the delightful menu. And she was attractive with a lovely, understated elegance. In short, she appeared to have it all. Her job, her family, and her home were all testimonies to her attention to detail and competence; and Helen had a smile for everyone. But Helen also had a secret that I never would have guessed. Helen was terribly lonely.

One day, when I had dashed out to the market in a pair of jeans and a sweatshirt because I was sure I could get in and out without seeing anyone I knew, I almost knocked over Helen with my shopping cart. I was studying my list while making a beeline for the cantaloupe. As I apologized, I saw something in her eyes I had never seen before—worry.

"Helen," I asked, "are you okay?" Once I said those words, I thought how ludicrous they must sound. Here was Helen in her color-coordinated silk outfit with every hair in place, whereas I was dressed in mismatched clothing and looked like

I was put together by a committee. But something about her expression made me pause.

"Well," she began hesitantly, "not really."

When her eyes filled with tears, I reached out to place my hand on her arm and said, "Hey, if you don't mind being seen with me, let's grab a cup of coffee in the bakery department." We pushed our carts to the cafe located in front of the bread display. As we settled at a small table with our steaming cups of coffee, she started to tell me some frightening news she had just received concerning the health of her oldest son.

I don't remember how long we sat there that morning, but I do remember it was the beginning of a difference in our relationship. For the first time I realized that Helen was a woman just like me. Despite her appearance and talents, she had doubts and fears too. Without realizing it, many women in my circle of friends had assumed that Helen was as "perfect" on the inside as she was on the outside; and because of our perceptions, and our own insecurities, we had distanced ourselves from her. We never stopped to think that she might need someone to talk to, to depend upon, to count on as a friend.

Helen and I see each other often now, and we laugh and talk about all kinds of things. She helped me learn how to arrange flowers; I taught her how to make pie crust from scratch. We've learned a lot from one another, but the most important thing we learned is that we need to look at people's hearts, not just their appearance. I still admire the beautiful picture she presents to the world, but now I respect even more the person I've come to know as a dear and trusted friend.

Radiate friendship and it will be returned tenfold.
—Henry P. Davidson

So Much for Solitude

Don Vieweg

work in a high-pressure advertising job, so years ago I began to spend my free time in lonely places where I didn't have to meet people. It wasn't that I didn't like them; it's just that I'd always been shy and I found that solitude helped me unwind. That's why I liked jogging; it provided solitude, and it helped me stay in shape too.

But one morning while I was jogging along West Shore Road in Conimicut, Rhode Island, and enjoying the bracing breeze of the Narragansett Bay shoreline, my attention was drawn to someone I'd only vaguely been aware of on other mornings. There was that same gaunt older woman again, walking alone on the other side of the road.

Curiosity got the better of me. For the first time, I crossed the road and found myself looking closely at her. She was walking slowly, staring sullenly at the ground, her arms wrapped tightly around her thin body as if holding herself apart from the world. Deep, sad lines cut across her face. She did not seem to notice me as I jogged by.

For days afterward I kept recalling that forlorn-looking woman. How defeated she had looked! How very lonely! "She looked as though she'd lost her last friend," I said to my wife, Dorothy.

I found myself praying for the woman, wondering about her, wondering if I would ever actually meet her. Then, despite my penchant for solitude, I began to hope I would meet her.

But what will I do if I meet her, Lord? I prayed. Meeting people had always been hard for me. I mean, wouldn't it be too forward to walk up and start talking to her?

At once the thought came to me: *smile at her.*

But no, I wanted to say, *smiling just isn't natural for me.* Ever since I was a teenager I've felt that my mouth isn't shaped right. My teeth aren't even and white. I've never liked my smile.

Smile, the thought came again.

Where had that thought come from? As a Christian I believe that God does speak to His children, but was that thought from Him?

Puzzled, I went into the bedroom and stood before the mirror, just as I'd done many times as a kid. I studied the face looking back at me. And just as I'd done back then, I decided to practice smiling.

It wasn't easy. I actually had to force myself. In the mirror, I saw the plaster of my face crack into a tentative, hopeful grin. With my cheek muscles I pulled that grin wider, feeling the jaw muscles tighten as I did so. It was more of a grimace than a smile.

I looked so ridiculous that I burst out laughing. But then I looked in the mirror again. At the tail end of the laugh—that was a real smile! When I wasn't trying so hard, the smile had occurred naturally!

Well, maybe I would try smiling after all, I thought.

But it was weeks before I encountered the gaunt woman again. There she was, her eyes staring straight ahead, her arms wrapped protectively about her chest.

I looked eagerly in her direction, gave her a good smile, and . . .

Nothing.

I don't think she even noticed. Overhead a seagull wheeled about, crying raucously.

My smile evaporated. I felt deflated.

But from somewhere deep within, a tiny voice seemed to prod me, saying, *Don't give up*. And I knew I mustn't. That woman seemed so lonely. It was important that she know someone cared.

The next time I encountered the woman was a few days later. She was still a block away when I spotted her walking toward me. It gave me time to work up an even better smile and to decide just what sort of greeting I would give.

She was still looking straight ahead as I approached. I found that smile and said cheerfully, "Good morning!"

Again, nothing.

Again and again over the following weeks the encounter was repeated.

"Hello!"

"Good morning!"

"Lovely day!"

The words were always mine. There was never a response. The only other sounds were the roaring of the surf and the pounding of my running shoes. Could anyone gain entrance to the woman's sad, silent world?

God, help me to reach her, I prayed that night.

"Good morning! Lovely day!" I shouted on our next encounter.

"Humpf!" she muttered, still staring stonily ahead.

But inside me, as I jogged on past, a kind of tension began to ease. *Praise God*, I thought. That "humpf" was like the opening of a door.

When I saw her again, she seemed different. Maybe it was my imagination, but it did seem to me that instead of her customary vacant stare, she actually recognized me. As I jogged closer, her arms were more relaxed and she was staring at me, her face puzzled.

"Good morning!" I shouted. "God bless you!"

She nodded. And there—ever so faintly—wasn't that a smile tugging at her lips? Yes! Yes, it was! I felt a sense of accomplishment as I jogged the remainder of my five miles that day.

The next time I saw her she was striding, head up, swinging her arms, looking boldly toward me.

"G—good morning," I choked.

"Morning," she replied softly, a timid smile on her lips.

Several days later we met again. This time her "Morning" was followed by a soft "Th—thank you!"

After that, the woman and I met frequently. I stopped to chat, first for a second or two, then longer. We had coffee, then several coffees. Her name was Pearl, and she needed someone to talk to.

Slowly, like the petals of a rose, she opened her life to me. Her husband had died ten years earlier. Her two married sons had moved across the country. Friends she had known had moved away too. She lived alone. And she confessed that she felt abandoned, hurt, angry, bitter.

"Until you started smiling at me, I thought no one in the world could ever care about me again," she said. "So I told myself I didn't care either. I didn't need anybody!"

After wiping her eyes, she continued, "But I learned from you what my wonderful husband had always tried to tell me: 'People really are nice, if you only give them a chance.'" Embarrassed, she looked down.

I took Pearl home and introduced her to Dorothy. They became friends too. We took her to church, where she began to make more friends.

And now when I'm jogging along West Shore Road, Pearl often flags me down, saying, "I've been waiting for you! I have so much to tell you!"

Well, so much for solitude. But I don't mind. It's just as Scripture says: "Give, and it shall be given unto you . . ." (Luke 6:38a). I gave Pearl friendship, and in return God used her to give me something too—a new way of living. I'm more outgoing now, and I like making friends.

All because of a smile.

Many a friendship—long, loyal and self-sacrificing—
rested at first upon no thicker a foundation
than a kind word.
—Frederick W. Faber

A Friend Like Patsy

Penney V. Schwab

*M*y friend Patsy and I usually sat on either end of the pew, sandwiching our wiggly preschoolers between us. Today we sat side by side. It was my last Sunday in the church we both loved. At dawn tomorrow our family was moving to a farm near Copeland, Kansas.

I'd miss the church and our friendly Texas town. I'd miss living just down the road from my husband Don's parents. But most of all, I'd miss my friends. Especially Patsy.

Patsy shared all the bits and pieces of my life. Every Thursday evening she sat at my kitchen table and poked strained carrots down six-month-old Rebecca while I taught her oldest sons to play my battered upright piano. We shared recipes: my fifty hamburger dinners (we raised beef) and Patsy's zillion ways with zucchini (she loved to garden).

We helped with each other's moneymaking projects. Patsy's "experiment" went great until we had to sort 500 creepy night crawlers from tubs of manure. My cattle-checking venture was fun—until we saw a diamondback rattler on a day we'd worn shorts and sandals to hunt for baby calves.

We team-taught the junior-high Sunday school class, provided oatmeal cookies for the Cherub Choir, and took our kids for picnics when our husbands worked late.

What would I do without Patsy?

She read my mind. "You'll make new friends right away," she whispered, squeezing my hand.

"Not like you," I whispered back, choking down the lump in my throat. I already knew there wouldn't be any friends like Patsy in Kansas. Everyone said so.

The elderly couple from whom we'd be renting the farmland said so. "My dear," they told me, "prepare to be very lonely. There simply aren't any young people around here."

My mother said so: "Small towns aren't always friendly to strangers." Don's mother said so: "It will be hard to meet anyone with you living eight miles out in the country. It's a good thing the children have each other for playmates."

The children had each other. Don had the farm. But what about me?

Patsy nudged my arm and we stood for the closing hymn, "What a Friend We Have in Jesus." I knew the Lord was my friend . . . and the most wonderful friend anyone could have. But I needed my earthly friends too!

Dear Lord, I prayed as the pastor gave the benediction, *please give me a friend just like Patsy.*

We set out for Kansas at seven o'clock on a chilly Monday morning in February. I drove our old white station wagon crammed with three children and a week's worth of clothing. A family friend loaded our furniture and appliances onto his truck, and also carried our German shepherds, Andi and Robert. Don's blue pickup brought up the rear. The back was piled with roped-down boxes of pots and pans, books and the baby bed. On the seat beside him, Don had a basket of green and yellow tissue-paper flowers—the last project Patsy and I had done together.

We were a modern-day wagon train. I was certain we were heading into hostile territory.

We arrived at the farm too late to begin unloading, so we spent the night at a motel in a neighboring town. The next day, we got the kind of Kansas welcome I'd dreaded. While we ate breakfast, light snowflakes turned into a snowstorm by noon and into a raging blizzard by early evening. Andi and Robert, disoriented by the snow, ran away.

I'd never felt so alone! I sank down on a soggy carton, one that was dripping melting snow all over the kitchen, and started to cry.

Then the telephone rang. I was so startled I let it ring again and again. Who could it be? I'd thought the line was still unconnected, and no one even knew we were here.

Finally I picked up the receiver. "Hello?"

"Welcome!" a friendly voice said. "I'm Audrey Button. I live in the yellow house two miles straight east. This weather is getting nasty, so I thought you might want to know how to use the phone, because it's an eight-party line, and who to call if you need help."

She gave me a list of numbers, then we visited for several minutes. Maybe this is the friend I prayed for, I thought, the one just like Patsy. But no. Mrs. Button's girls were grown and gone, and she and her husband were semiretired. She was nice but not at all like Patsy.

After two days of snow, the weather warmed up. I discovered there was something worse than being snowbound: we were now marooned by mud. Our two and a half miles of dirt road (heavy clay soil at that) dissolved into an impassable quagmire.

That's why we were surprised when, about nine o'clock one night, there was a knock at the door. "We're Howard and Ruth Stude," a pleasant, middle-aged couple introduced themselves. "We're your third-to-nearest neighbors." They apologized for coming so late and explained they'd been afraid to try our roads before they froze semisolid.

"We hope you'll come to our church," Ruth invited.

"We'll see," I hedged. The church she described sounded nice, but it couldn't possibly be like the one I'd left.

We went that Sunday anyway. The people were friendly and the building was lovely. There were two little girls Patrick's age and twins who were nearly four, like Michael. But no babies, and no one who looked like a replacement for Patsy.

That week I went to Copeland's one small grocery store. The aisles were very narrow, and Rebecca amused herself by grabbing things from one side while I was on the other—a box of oatmeal while I was searching for rice, a can of beans while I stocked up on corn. And she did it all from the seat of the shopping cart.

I was afraid I'd be banned. But Annie and Edith, the proprietors, just laughed. "We've been thinking of building a bigger grocery," Edith said. "If your baby is going to be a regular customer, we'll do it for sure!"

Annie made a sign about my dogs: Lost south of Copeland, two silver German shepherds. She posted it in the front window. (A week later the dogs were home, safe and sound.)

On my next visit to town I noticed a tiny building of corrugated tin right underneath the water tower. Copeland Public Library, a white sign read, Hours 2–5, Tuesday and Thursday.

Since it was 2:30 p.m. on Thursday, I went in. The librarian was a frail woman with sparkling blue eyes and hair as gray as the building.

"I'm new here," I told her. "Can I apply for a library card without having someone cosign it?" (My old library required two character references.)

"My dear, choose as many books as you like!" the librarian said. "Just sign your name on each card."

I chose three and took them to the desk. She stamped them, then indicated a chair next to her. "I'm Mrs. Ewing," she said. "If you have time, tell me about yourself."

We had a wonderful visit—the first of many. But much as I liked her, she wasn't the right age to be another Patsy.

Several weeks passed. My closest neighbor, Neva Patterson, held a get-acquainted coffee for Don and me. It was loads of fun, and I met many interesting people. But not one could replace Patsy.

When Patsy called to see how I was adjusting, I told her so. "I've met lots of lovely people," I said, "but they're all too old, or they don't have kids the ages of mine, or we aren't interested in the same things."

"So what?" Patsy replied. "You and I aren't the same age, and we didn't have much in common when we first met. You liked sports, I liked sewing. You read mysteries, I preferred romances. You liked comedies, I went for long, sad movies."

Funny, I'd forgotten all that. I'd forgotten that my friendship with Patsy had developed slowly and deepened over a period of years.

"You'll never have another friend like me," Patsy continued, "because I'm one of a kind. God only makes originals, you know. No carbon copies."

No carbon copies!

In my search for a friend "just like Patsy," I'd overlooked the many "originals" God had sent my way. People like Mrs. Ewing, the store ladies, my wonderful neighbors. Friendship, I realized as Patsy and I said good-bye, wasn't a matter of age or family or common interests. It was sharing, and caring, and growing together. And it rarely came instantly.

God had been answering my prayers for a friend since our first day in Copeland. He'd brought a whole community of people into my life. In time, I'd have friendships just as beautiful and deep as the one Patsy and I shared.

*There is nothing we like to see so much as the gleam of
pleasure in a person's eye when he feels that we have
sympathized with him, understood him,
interested ourself in his welfare.*

—DON MARQUIS

STANDING ON COMMON GROUND

MAYO MATHERS

The screams outside startled me awake. I stumbled
across the room to peer through the curtains. A man
snatched a baby from a woman's arms. A knife flashed in the
darkness. The neighbors were having another fight.

Unable to sleep, I thought longingly of our home in Oregon,
where neighbors clipped coupons and attended PTA meetings.
Here in this apartment in inner-city Anchorage, Alaska, my neighbors were prostitutes, thieves, and drug dealers.

A recession back home in central Oregon had brought our
well-drilling business to a halt. All around us, people in the construction business were filing for bankruptcy. We wanted to
avoid such a drastic step, yet as our savings account dwindled,
we knew our only hope lay in a temporary relocation.

Hearing stories of a booming economy in Alaska, we withdrew the rest of our savings, loaded our pickup, and headed
north. In Anchorage we found that high rents limited our
choices. We took the first apartment within our budget.

As we settled into our new surroundings, I worried about the
influence this neighborhood would have on our family. Our two
sons, Tyler and Landon, were used to sagebrush and rabbits. Now
a paved street would be their play area. And what about friendship?
How could I, a homemaker, become friends with a prostitute?

We attended a small church that eagerly welcomed us. Among these people I found the normalcy I missed from home. I joined a weekly Bible study group and decided to fulfill my need for friendship through the church.

The Lord seemed to have other ideas. Every time I opened the Bible, I stumbled on passages such as *"I was hungry and you gave me nothing to eat, I was thirsty and you gave me nothing to drink, I was a stranger and you did not invite me in"* (Matthew 25:42–43, NIV).

The idea of inviting these neighbors into my home filled me with unease. "What on earth would we talk about, Lord?" I argued as I prayed. "We have no common ground."

Still, I could not forget those Bible passages.

I decided the easiest place to start would be with the children. I encouraged our sons to invite the neighborhood kids to join us for "Bible snacks." Each evening I made a plate of snacks, which we ate while we read Bible stories. Word spread, and soon everyone wanted to take part in our Bible snacks.

This gave me a chance to get acquainted with the children. As they became comfortable in our home, they spent more time there. I felt easier about this than having Tyler and Landon play in the street with them. In my house I could oversee John, who was a bully, make sure Mercedes wasn't being teased, and monitor the games Raoul invented.

One night a boy I hadn't seen before rang our doorbell. "Is it time for Bible snack?" he asked.

Nodding, I invited him in and asked his name. "Bobby," he said, and held up a pillowcase full of dirty clothes. "My mom told me to spend the night with you. She said you'd wash my clothes too."

As I sorted through the tattered clothing, tears splashed

onto the hopelessly soiled fabric. I had never met Bobby's mother; I didn't know where he lived. I raged against the injustice of children shouldering the burden of their own upbringing.

By now I had begun to embrace the challenge the neighborhood presented. One afternoon I invited Crystal, the Hispanic woman next door, over for coffee. Her eager acceptance surprised me. As we talked she told me she had abandoned a husband and four children to pursue dancing. Her career faltered; in desperation, she turned to prostitution. Now she longed to return to her family, but shame held her captive.

The next day I introduced myself to Josie, a black woman from Georgia who was married to a drug dealer. She refused to come inside; instead, she perched hesitantly on the back doorstep, ready to run the minute she heard her husband's demanding voice. Over coffee she spoke of how well he treated her. Nighttime, however, told a different story. Their fights echoed through the darkness, and their children flinched when I reached out to touch them.

Then there was Scarlett. She had a history of marriages—with a child from each one. She and her present husband earned their living by selling goods stolen during nightly raids on more affluent neighborhoods. About once a month Scarlett rang my doorbell. "God told me to tell you I have no food for my kids. Can you lend me some money?" On these occasions I phoned shelters, then drove her around to pick up food from them.

There were others in the diverse group living around us, and I eventually formed tentative friendships with many of them. Though they never invited me to their apartments, they frequently came to mine. As they shared bits of their private lives, I was staggered by the hopelessness of their situations. Yet I found each woman had a dream she clung to stubbornly.

Though each dream was different, the ending was the same one we all long for: happily ever after.

At last the long dark winter began to fade. Spring peeked shyly through lingering mounds of snow. One day dawned so warm and sunny that I sat on my doorstep soaking in the golden warmth. Shortly, Crystal came bounding out to join me and we chatted casually. Before long, Josie came up the walk. She hesitated over my invitation to join us, having suffered many times from Crystal's outspoken bigotry. But she decided to take the risk.

Gradually other women were tempted from behind the safety of their doors. I was amazed. I had never known these women to visit together. When they came to my apartment, they always made certain I was alone. Now, as I listened to the hum of their voices around me, I studied their faces—Eskimo, Spanish, Korean, black, white, prostitute, abused wife, drug addict, homemaker. Somehow we had stumbled onto common ground: the bond of motherhood. We had all experienced childbirth, teething, and potty training. I was listening to the same chatter I had heard countless times back in Oregon. Mrs. Tangabooluk shared the Eskimo cure for colic; Sung Li gave us Korean advice on teething; Crystal talked about her desire to establish contact with her children.

These women nurtured the same dreams for their children that I did for mine. They shared the same sense of vulnerability I had when my kids were hurt. I began to see these women from a new perspective. Until now, my association with them had been based on pity, and maybe even a sense of superiority. A new emotion came over me: admiration. These mothers were carrying out their responsibilities despite giant handicaps.

I never had to ask someone for food to feed my children,

or protect them from drug deals going on in my home. What kind of mother would I have been under those conditions?

Soon after, the economy back in Oregon improved, and we packed our bags. The sadness I felt as I said good-bye took me by surprise. The day we left, Crystal brought me a parting gift—a pair of high-heeled velvet slippers trimmed in soft pink fur. Rhinestones twinkled on the toes. I packed them beside my worn tennis shoes, delighted by the contrast.

The slippers were not the only gift I received. I had been given the ability to see into the women's hearts, which had been hidden behind their circumstances. I had learned to look beyond the tattered clothes of the children and see their distinctive personalities: John, the leader; Raoul, the organizer; Mercedes, the peacemaker. God had a plan for their lives just as He had for ours.

I caught a glimpse of His plan as Crystal and I hugged good-bye. "I'm going to be leaving here too," she whispered. I looked at her in astonishment. "I know it won't be easy, but I've decided to go home—back to my family. Will you pray for me?"

I smiled. Of course I would. We were standing on common ground.

Friends are a second existence.
—BALTASAR GRACIÁN Y MORALES

SAILING STEERAGE TO NEW YORK
WALTER ALLEN

I remember that on the second or third day—we were out of Belfast and steaming past the shores of Northern Ireland—having realized that crowded though we were everyone else was ignoring the lack of privacy and making himself at home, I plucked up courage to take out my fiddle and play softly to myself.

I was in fact murdering Beethoven's first violin sonata as usual. I was sitting on my bunk, which was in the bottom tier, as I played, and I was suddenly aware of a man standing above me gesticulating furiously. I had already marked him down as a fellow to be avoided, for his aspect seemed to me villainous. He was a huge man, whose face, except for his tiny eyes and red bulbous nose that looked as though it had been shoved on as an afterthought, was almost wholly obscured by a shaggy beard. He was dressed in the most outlandish garments, in a Russian peasant blouse, his feet and legs bound up in rags. He was a man I shrank from, and there he was, seemingly about to snatch my fiddle from me by its neck and then standing back and playing an imaginary violin in pantomime and, that done, jerking his thumb furiously at his chest. It took me a little time to gather what he meant, and then, so enormously did he loom above me and so ferocious did he appear, there seemed nothing for it but to hand him the instrument.

He stared at it with delight. In those great hairy hands it

looked like a toy fiddle. I was in agony lest he should break it, for
to tell the truth, I no more regarded the fellow as human than if
he had been a gorilla. But his face was lit up with joy, and with
two strides he was in the middle of the steerage, the fiddle tucked
beneath his worn doormat of a beard, and the bow on the strings
was making music of a kind I had never heard before. It was wild,
passionate, and melancholy; I found it almost physically frightening for it seemed to pluck at a nerve in my stomach. It was most
decidedly not Beethoven's first sonata; it was not to my mind civ-
ilized at all but an expression of primitive and intense melancholy.

As he played, quietness fell on the steerage. Everyone was
listening, and after a time some of the passengers began to
dance, and again it was a dance the like of which I have not seen
before or since. For years I was haunted by this music my friend,
for the loan of the instrument made him my friend, conjured
from my fiddle. . . . It was not until quite recent years, with the
coming of wireless, that I heard anything like it again, and then
I realized it was Tzigane music, the music of the Hungarian
gypsies, but played by my friend with a barbaric pathos and
splendor beyond anything I ever heard on the BBC.

He was my first friend. When he returned the fiddle to me
I gave him to understand that he could use it whenever he liked.
To my embarrassment, he embraced me. But thereafter we spent
much of the day together. We could converse only by smile and
gesture, for his language was beyond me entirely, and though he
told me what I assumed was his name, I could not pronounce it.
He on his side managed "Billy" very satisfactorily, and no sooner
was I under his protection than I was "Billy" to all the members
of his national group, whatever it was, and they made me richly
welcome. For my part, I felt both proud and safe with this
uncouth giant, who was the slave of gratitude, at my side.

Acts of Friendship

It is not the services we render them, but the services they render us, that attaches people to us.

−LABICHE ET MARTIN

MORE THAN A PAINTING

JEFFREY MINICK

*D*uring the longest summer of my life—the summer of '92—there was a painting of my house hanging in the gallery across Main Street from our bookshop. Friends kept stopping by, asking, "Have you seen the painting? It's beautiful."

My wife, Kris, returned from the gallery impressed. "I wish your mom could see it," she said. "You know how she loves the house."

Mom, sadly, was too ill to leave her home, and I was busy helping take care of her. But one afternoon in early August I went to the gallery to take a look. The walls were drenched with color, filled with beautiful depictions of our town—Main Street, walkways, gardens, older homes.

Then I saw the painting. Though many people had photographed, sketched, or painted our turn-of-the-century house, no one had captured its whimsical character the way that artist, Ann Vasilik, had. She had shown it from what might be considered its ugly side, where the stack pipes and rambling renovations were visible. But in Ann's soft, warm colors, our house looked just as I fancied it—a dowager in genteel poverty, her fortunes down but her pride undiminished.

As I studied the picture, I felt for the first time in weeks an interest in something other than my own troubles. But one glance at the price told me the painting was beyond the means of a small-town bookseller.

The summer had begun on a high note. I had finally decided to make a major commitment to my faith and join the Catholic church. Just a week later, however, I got some terrible news: my mother was dying of cancer. Ever since, I had lived in a haze, as if the world's sights and sounds came to me through gauze.

I left the art gallery without giving the painting further thought. In the midst of making Mom's last days comfortable, I didn't even notice when the exhibit closed.

After Mom's death in early September, I settled into a routine that helped me get through each day. Prayer brought me some comfort, but my grief went deeper than I imagined possible. Without Mom—the soul, the center of our family—I felt overwhelmed by the dark forces that accompany grief . . . loneliness, emptiness, despair, and isolation.

In November our good friends Henry and Julie Nathan asked us to supper at their house. Kris and I were surprised at the large buffet spread out in the dining room. Julie explained that she had invited a few other friends to join us. We chatted in the living room, greeting others as they entered.

As more and more guests arrived, anxiety gripped me. This wasn't a small party. The room was filling with people. Although they were all friends of ours, I couldn't make the connection between some of them and the Nathans. Why were they there?

Never before had I felt such an extraordinary tension in the air, a sense of an impending event. Finally, Julie came into the room with a large object wrapped in a blanket. "Attention, everyone!" she called. Then she turned to Kris and me: "We all chipped in to get it for you."

Julie whisked away the cloth. There was a watercolor, like a bright jewel, all sunlight and shimmering warmth. I was so overwhelmed it took me several seconds to realize it was the painting of our house.

The rest of that evening remains vague in my memory. Our friends applauded. I got to my feet and stammered a few remarks of gratitude. My wife cried. I scarcely remember eating supper or visiting afterward.

What I vividly recall, however, was an amazing sense of blessing, of knowing God's grace was at work. For weeks I had thought I was alone, cut off from others, yet here was proof of the love and friendship that filled my life.

Today the watercolor hangs above the mantel in our living room. Guests often ask about it, and then I gladly tell them how it came to me. I never tire of the story. Because each time I tell it, I look at the painting and see not simply a picture of my house. I see instead the faces of my friends.

A friend should bear his friend's infirmities.
—William Shakespeare

Neighbor in Need

Flora Reigada

The first sign that Anna and her family didn't fit in in our well-kept neighborhood came the day after the moving van left. The bikes and trikes that had been unloaded still littered the lawn and sidewalk at sundown. They weren't put away in the garage or moved to the backyard where people wouldn't trip over them. They stayed where the children dropped them, and Anna (at least that's the name I'm using here) didn't seem in a hurry to pick them up.

That was unusual in our Washington, D.C.-area subdivision. It was a neat bedroom community of ranch houses and colonials. Most of the owners had good jobs with the federal government. Our kids played together in the cul-de-sac or nearby woods, and they all attended the same local school. Neighbors didn't hesitate to borrow a stick of butter or a cup of sugar. We were all in the same boat. Not rich by any means, but respectable.

Our own two-story colonial came complete with wall-to-wall carpeting and a full basement with washer and dryer. It was the first time I'd owned a brand-new home, and I was proud. Maybe that's why I felt so uneasy when Anna's garden sprouted weeds and the lawn grew cowlicks. Her kids seemed a little too rambunctious.

"How many children does that poor woman have?" I overheard one neighbor say in the supermarket.

"At least five," another responded. "I haven't finished counting."

"No wonder she doesn't have time to pick up after them," the other said, without much sympathy.

One day I peered out my kitchen window and spotted Anna with her five children (indeed there were five—four marching behind her like ducklings, the baby on her hip) headed to our house. I wiped my hands on my apron and rushed to the door. "Come in," I said. They all traipsed inside, and I poured Anna a cup of coffee.

"Would you like any candy?" I offered the youngest daughter, who turned to her mother with a questioning look.

"Yes, you may," Anna said. I opened a bag of hard candies, and the next thing I knew four grubby hands plunged into it like trick-or-treaters on a binge. "Thank you, thank you, thank you!" they shouted, and then ran off to play with my three children.

"Don't you just love kids?" Anna said, and let out a belly laugh. She bounced her baby on her lap. She was a big, blowsy woman with striking red hair, and as we chatted, I discovered she was bright and perfectly pleasant to talk to. *Maybe I've misjudged her,* I thought. When we began to discuss churches in the area, I wondered if she and I might start a Bible study group.

She was nursing her baby when she said, almost as an aside, "Every day I thank God for government assistance. Without it we'd never be able to rent a house in this neighborhood."

A chill went through me. This woman and her family were living off the government. A welfare mom in our subdivision! This was a place where people owned their houses—they didn't rent. Chattering away blithely, Anna told me far more than I wanted to know about food stamps, entitlements, and her husband, on disability because of a stress disorder. I didn't want to hear it.

I would have avoided Anna after that, but in the close confines of the neighborhood, it simply wasn't possible. Our children hung out together, building forts in the woods and dams along the stream, playing kick the can on summer nights when the fireflies flickered in the dusk. In the morning, Anna would drop by for a cup of coffee, the baby in her arms.

In her bighearted way, she was good company, discussing her faith, laughing over the antics of her kids. She was a good mother to them—loving and firm. But then I'd think of how hard Dan, my husband, worked so that we could have our house. Every morning he was up at 6:00 AM to drive to his job, and he was rarely home before dark. Anna's husband, on the other hand, could be found sitting on their stoop in the middle of the day.

That he was disabled didn't seem an excuse. My own father had been disabled, but it didn't prevent my mother from working as a switchboard operator to provide for us. At sixteen, I quit school to take a job and help out. We would never have accepted aid. The faint glow of good feeling I'd had toward Anna soon dissipated into a chilly cloud of disapproval. Whenever I started to laugh at one of her jokes or look forward to discussing a Bible verse with her, it was as though an icy curtain came clanging down. Where in the Bible did it say we could be freeloaders?

One April morning Anna called. "Flora, I'm in a terrible bind. My usual sitter can't make it, and I have a doctor's appointment this afternoon. Could you come over?"

What about your husband? I thought. "Okay," I said hesitantly. "If you can't find anybody else."

I had never balanced so many children at once—my three plus Anna's five and everyone else's in the neighborhood running in and out. If I wasn't changing diapers or pouring juice, I was inspecting a skinned knee or reminding someone to close a door. Sinking down on the sofa, I wondered how Anna managed. Just then she came in the door, radiant.

"Good news!" she exclaimed. "I'm pregnant."

I almost blurted out, "How could you?" but didn't. Inside, though, the judgments flew. *How irresponsible can she be!*

Throughout her pregnancy Anna kept visiting me. It was easy to get caught up in the excitement of a new baby—picking out names, planning a shower, taking old baby clothes out of storage. I kept reminding myself, though, who had probably paid for those clothes, who would really be supporting this child.

That December Anna gave birth to a healthy, eight-pound, ten-ounce boy she named Matthew. "His name means gift from God," she said. "Isn't he perfect?" And, of course, he was—a perfect gift from God.

Shortly after Matthew's birth, I caught a virus I couldn't shake. "You're exhausted," the doctor said. "You need complete rest." He insisted I stay off my feet. *With three children and a husband who works all day,* I wondered, *how can I?* I kept getting up to do laundry, cook, and clean, which only made me feel worse. Energy seeped from me like air escaping through a slow leak in a tire.

One day I was sacked out on the couch, dirty dishes piled in the sink and grimy clothes spilling from the laundry basket, when Anna dropped by, a sleeping Matthew in her arms. She took one look at me and exclaimed, "Why didn't you call and tell me you were sick?"

"Why would I?" I mumbled. "You have enough to deal with on your own."

"That doesn't mean I can't help you," she said cheerfully. It was as if she were energized by my need. She tucked little Matthew in a blanket and nested him on the couch close to me, then rolled up her sleeves. She washed my dishes, did all the laundry, tidied up, and cooked a casserole for my family's dinner. Then day after day she came by to lend a hand or just cheer me up.

One morning while Anna was busy in my kitchen, I opened my Bible to the parable of the good Samaritan. The good Samaritan—the good neighbor—was the one who actually stopped and asked, "What can I do to help?"

Yes, Anna took. But she also gave. There were others in the neighborhood who might have rallied around me, but Anna was the one who rolled up her sleeves and pitched in wholeheartedly. If we were such a nice community, why had none of us helped her get back on her feet? Maybe we'd been too busy complaining about her messy yard that our kids loved to play in.

I'm thankful, God, that you've sent me Anna, I thought, then stiffened. I personally didn't approve of her taking government handouts, and I doubted I ever would. I had certain principles, and I felt I was right. But somehow I now realized a bigger issue was at stake, a spiritual issue. I sensed God saying to me, *Flora, it is more important to love than to be "right."*

"Anna," I called to her. She appeared in the doorway carrying a bowl of macaroni and cheese for one of my kids.

"I just wanted to tell you," I said. "You're a good neighbor. I hope I can be one to you too."

Eventually Anna and her family moved away to make a new start in another part of the country, and "order" was restored to our neighborhood. Yet I found myself missing the messy yard and the clamor of her brood. I missed Anna. No, she didn't change my views on government policy. But she changed my idea of what it is to be a good neighbor.

There is a friend that sticketh closer than a brother.
—PROVERBS 18:24B

FRIENDS TO THE RESCUE

DENNIS MATHIS

*I*f there is one thing I've learned as a building contractor, it's this: Expect the unexpected. All sorts of things can and do go wrong: your materials aren't delivered, the weather turns on you, your workers get sick. You really don't know what to expect until you've rolled up your sleeves and dug into the job. Even the most straightforward project, I tell people, has the capacity to trip you up. There's an old expression: "Men plan, God laughs." That sure feels true sometimes in construction work.

But this is the story of the complete opposite—the one-in-a-million job where everything goes right.

It begins one Sunday in the fall of 1998 when we heard at church that one of our members, Steve Orme, had been diagnosed with cancer and needed our prayers. My wife, Robin, and I went up to Steve and his wife, Linda, after services and let them know that if there was anything they needed, anything at all, we were there. "Thanks, you two," Linda said, giving us each a hug. "Just keep praying."

I wondered, though, if there was more we could do. You worry sometimes that when friends are in trouble they hesitate to ask for more worldly assistance.

A few weeks later I was finishing a job in Steve and Linda's neighborhood when I saw Linda out on her front steps. I stopped and asked her again how I could help. She seemed a little embarrassed by my question but replied, "Well, could you give me a quote on some work? Steve had started redoing the upstairs before he got sick . . . "

"You bet," I said. "Let's go take a look right now."

I turned off the ignition and followed her inside as she explained that Steve had felt well enough to go into work for a few hours today. "I have to warn you," she said, pausing at the foot of the stairs, "it's a bit of a mess up there."

"Don't worry, I'm unshockable," I laughed, trying to reassure her.

But when we reached the children's bedroom, I couldn't believe what a shambles the place was. The room was piled high with boxes. Scrape marks crisscrossed the ceiling where the finish had been. Closet doors had been taken off and leaned against the walls. The carpet and padding had been removed, the plywood lying bare and covered by tacks.

Inside the bathroom, a hole in the wall looked straight down into the garage. "This isn't so bad, Linda," I fibbed.

"Well," she said, "let me show you the master bedroom."

It was worse than the kids' room. Suddenly I pictured Steve lying on his back in bed, weak and exhausted from chemotherapy, staring up at the dreary, water-stained ceiling.

"What do you think?" said Linda.

"No trouble at all," I told her brightly.

"Well," she said, "here's the thing. My brother gave us his frequent-flyer miles and we were hoping to get away to Seattle for twelve days over Christmas and New Year's, just the kids and us, before Steve begins his next round of chemo. I was wondering if there was any way you could finish the work then as a surprise for Steve."

"No problem, Linda," I said.

"How much will it set us back?"

"Don't worry about it," I told her.

"No, Dennis, really."

"No big deal," I said, knowing full well what I was taking on. "I have subcontractors who owe me. We'll work something out. I don't want you guys to be worrying about money at a time like this."

That's when Linda broke down. She told me how upset Steve was about all the unfinished work, how the worry about the house hung over him when he needed all his strength to get better.

"You just let me know when I can start," I said.

At home that night I described the situation to Robin and our five children. "The upstairs is a huge mess but I've got an idea. We could finish everything ourselves as a Christmas project while they're away."

"Well," said Robin, digging in eagerly. "A lot of people have been asking how they can help the Ormes." Then Robin got a gleam in her eye. "In fact," she said, "if enough people got involved, I'll bet we could redo their whole house!" The kids voted unanimously to pitch in however they could.

That was a lot more work than I had in mind, but over the next weeks, as I talked to friends from church, everyone seemed to want to lend a hand. Linda's best friend, Duan Harding, dropped by the Ormes' house to quickly itemize a list of needs. An accountant set up a fund into which people could contribute. An elderly man offered to coordinate the volunteers. "I've got lots of time," he said. "I'm retired." Amazingly, as word of our plans got around, businesses I worked with offered supplies at cost.

I worried that the huge extent of what we were planning would get back to the Ormes. Steve had already learned that I was going to do some work on the upstairs. I didn't want him—or Linda—to find out about the rest, the new kitchen and carpeting, the tiled floors, the upgraded electrical wiring. They didn't need to know that practically the whole congregation and a lot of their neighbors were in on it now.

As for me, I was getting more excited each day. "It'll be a race against the clock," I told Robin shortly before Steve, Linda, and their kids were to fly to Seattle, "but I still think we can do it."

"Remember how this started," Robin reminded me. "With prayer. God is guiding our plans, Dennis. He brought all these people together."

"Let's just hope that Steve's healing is part of God's plan too," I said, suddenly reminded that the battle our friend faced was far graver than any of our problems.

As soon as the Ormes left on Wednesday, two days before Christmas, we moved in. We had twelve days to create a whole new home. Volunteers swarmed over the house, day and night, moving furniture, tearing up carpet, hauling away the old gas range and kitchen sink. We got rid of the tub and the sink and the tiles in the bathroom. As fast as it all went out, new fixtures and appliances came in. Ceilings were replastered, walls painted and papered, floors carpeted and retiled. Each day when we paused for meals, we always said a special prayer for Steve and his family.

On Friday, Christmas Day arrived, crisp and cool for California. After Robin and I and our five kids opened presents, the two older boys and I planned to drive down to the ocean to go surfing before dinner, a tradition with us. But we decided to spend the day working on the Orme house instead. Afterward the boys swore it was the happiest Christmas of their life.

The work continued all week right up to the hour that the

Ormes were due home on January 4th. A church youth group finished resodding the lawn while their mothers sewed curtains for the bedroom. A neighbor showed up and installed a new electric garage door. Someone else split a cord of wood for the fireplace. Standing back and looking at the sign some of them had hung over the front stairs—*Welcome Home! We Love You!*— I couldn't help but feel awed and humbled by how smoothly the incredible effort had gone.

Surely no amount of effort seemed too great to any of us when we saw Steve's reaction at the sight of an entirely refurbished home, the home he had worried so much about as he fought against a terrible illness. As the throng closed around them, Linda started hugging everyone in sight and Robin took my hand in hers. Soon the whole wonderful, unbelievable scene became a blur to me behind a cloud of tears.

Yes, I try to expect the unexpected, but I could never have expected this, the incredible joy that helping and caring brought to everyone.

*Actions, not words, are the true criterion
of the attachment of friends.*
—GEORGE WASHINGTON

STITCHES IN TIME

ROBERTA MESSNER

I found them in the attic while rummaging through a trunk. Several years before, I had tucked away vintage samplers that I had gathered from antiques shops and garage sales. Now I spread them out with pleasure, reading the sayings that exhorted the virtues of patience and patriotism, work and life's simple joys. As I scanned my collection, I envisioned a doting grandmother hovering over her granddaughter, teaching her skills for life—reading, arithmetic, and the needle arts.

Stepping back into the past for a few minutes was just what I needed. For days I had been feeling frustrated. I hadn't been able to do anything to cheer up my coworker Cathy, and it was on my mind. As we worked together at the hospital, Cathy had talked about caring for her terminally ill mother, and I could see the sadness in her eyes. It made my heart heavy: Why couldn't I think of any way to help Cathy?

TO HAVE A FRIEND

YOU MUST FIRST BE ONE

I looked again at my array of samplers. My small collection spanned more than a century, and each work was as personal as a fingerprint. I knew that samplers had been used in Colonial times as educational tools, and the folk and religious wisdom they imparted had been part of a young woman's upbringing. As years passed, samplers had served more decorative purposes;

some were sparked with whimsy, and others had a charm that clearly reflected the personality of the seamstress.

I unearthed a box of dusty old picture frames and matched the samplers to the appropriate size, shape, and design, envisioning just the place to hang them in a downstairs hallway. The next morning I carried my box of nostalgia to the local framing shop, eagerly awaiting the results.

A week later I picked up the framed samplers. As I turned to leave the shop, the owner stopped me. "A businessman visiting from a nearby city happened to be in here the other day and noticed one of your samplers," she told me. "He said his mother is seriously ill, and that verse reminded him of her. He wondered if you would be willing to sell it."

I gazed at the one she was pointing to:

MOTHER'S LOVE

IS LIKE A FRAGRANT ROSE

WITH SWEETNESS IN EVERY FOLD

I remembered when a lady at a flea market had told me to dab lemon juice and salt on the old stained linen and place it in the sun. The refurbished beauty was one of my favorites, and I had no intention of parting with it. But to be polite, I jotted down the name—William Eads—and his phone number.

The next day as I surveyed my treasures, my eye fell on this message:

IT IS IN LOVING

NOT IN BEING LOVED

THE HEART IS BLESSED

How loving was I being if I didn't at least speak to William Eads? Somewhat reluctantly, I dialed his number several times that evening but got no answer. "I've done my part," I reassured myself in relief. "Now I'll get to work in peace." I planned and measured for my arrangement, then carefully drove the nails into the wall.

But as I raised the "Mother" sampler, I found I was unable to lower it to its position on the nail. I gazed again at the fragile cross-stitching of threads forming the complete picture. For a moment it seemed the stitches almost came alive with the vitality of the fingers that had lovingly made them. Fingers whose activity conveyed a sense of commitment, shared an honest sentiment. . . .

Maybe this sampler was meant to be shared.

The next morning, before I left for work, I dialed the number again. William Eads answered. "You don't know who I am," I explained, "but the owner of the framing shop told me your mother is very ill. . . ."

He knew immediately who I was. "Would it be possible to buy that sampler from you?" he asked. "It reminds me so much of my mother. She adores samplers. She used to work on them herself until she became too sick." He paused and took a breath. "And her love—just as the sampler says—is like a rose."

Suddenly I was flooded with thoughts of the sweet-smelling roses my own mother once tended. "I want to give it to you," I blurted out. "Tell me your address and I'll mail it."

LET ME LIVE IN A HOUSE

BY THE SIDE OF THE ROAD

AND BE A FRIEND TO MAN

"I can't tell you how much I appreciate this," the man said excitedly. "But you don't need to mail it. I'll be visiting my mother this weekend, and she lives close to you. Would you mind leaving the sampler at her house?"

He gave me directions to his mother's home. I quickly wrapped the sampler in a brown paper sack and dashed off to deliver it before heading to work.

I pulled up in front of a brick split-level home. When I rang the bell, a middle-aged lady came to the door. She explained that Mrs. Eads was unable to leave her bed. I introduced myself and handed her the package. "It's from Mrs. Eads's son," I said, eagerly handing her my parcel. It suddenly felt wonderful to have given something I loved to a perfect stranger.

Later that day I spotted my friend Cathy walking across the hospital grounds. When I greeted her, she gave me a smile more cheerful than I had seen in weeks. "So what sort of strange men were you telephoning earlier today?" she asked playfully.

I looked at her in astonishment. How did she know what I had been doing?

"Does the name William Eads ring a bell?" Cathy asked. I nodded.

"He's my brother," she said. "Eads was my maiden name. And you just delivered that sampler to my mother. My brother called and told me about your visit and your gift." Cathy explained how touched her mother had been when she saw the sampler that had meant so much to William. "I can't wait to see it," she said.

For a moment I stood staring at her, then I broke into a beaming smile of my own.

WARM FRIENDSHIP

LIKE THE SETTING SUN SHINES

KINDLY LIGHT ON EVERYONE

Little stitches, little gestures. Stitch after stitch, hand over hand. And on it goes, over the years, in gestures of caring and love.

How do you make a sampler yours for keeps? By feeling its message in your heart and sharing that message with others.

In time of great anxiety we can draw
power from our friends.
—D. LUPTON

A SMALL TRAGEDY

AGNES REPPLIER

I was twelve years old and very happy in my convent
school. I did not particularly mind studying my lessons,
and I sometimes persuaded the less experienced nuns to accept
a retentive memory as a substitute for intelligent understanding,
with which it had nothing to do. I "got along" with the other
children, and I enjoyed my friends; and of such simple things is
the life of a child composed.

Then came a disturbing letter from my mother, a letter
which threatened the heart of my content. It was sensible and
reasonable, and it said very plainly and very kindly that I had
better not make an especial friend of Lilly Milton; "not an
exclusive friend," wrote my mother, "not one whom you would
expect to see immediately after you leave school."

I knew what all that meant. I was as innocent as a kitten;
but divorces were not common in those conservative years, and
Mrs. Milton had as many to her credit as if she were living—a
highly esteemed and popular lady—today. I regretted my
mother's tendency to confuse issues with unimportant details (a
mistake which grown-up people often made), and I felt sure
that if she knew Lilly—who was also as innocent as a kitten and
was blessed with the sweetest temper that God ever gave a little
girl—she would be delighted that I had such an excellent friend.
So I went on happily enough until ten days later, when
Madame Rayburn, a nun for whom I cherished a very warm

affection, was talking to me upon a familiar theme—the diverse ways in which I might improve my classwork and my general behavior. The subject did not interest me deeply—repetition had staled its vivacity—until my companion said the one thing that had plainly been uppermost in her mind: "And Agnes, how did you come to tell Lilly Milton that your mother did not want you to go with her? I never thought you could have been so deliberately unkind."

This brought me to my feet with a bound. "Tell Lilly!" I cried. "You could not have believed such a thing. It was Madame Bouron who told her."

A silence followed this revelation. The convent discipline was as strict for the nuns as for the pupils, and it was not their custom to criticize their superiors. Madame Bouron was mistress general, ranking next to the august head, and of infinitely more importance to us. She was a cold, severe, sardonic woman, and the general dislike for her had shaped itself into a cult. I had accepted this cult in simple good faith, having no personal grudge until she did this dreadful thing; and I may add that it was the eminently unwise custom of reading all the letters written to or by the pupils which stood responsible for the trouble. The order of nuns was a French one, and the habit of surveillance, which did not seem amiss in France, was ill-adapted to America. I had never before wasted a thought upon it. My weekly home letter and the less frequent but more communicative epistles from my mother might have been read in the market place for all I cared, until this miserable episode proved that a bad usage may be trusted to produce, sooner or later, bad results.

It was with visible reluctance that Madame Rayburn said after a long pause: "That alters the case. If Madame Bouron told Lilly, she must have had some good reason for doing so."

"There was no good reason," I protested. "There couldn't have been. But it doesn't matter. I told Lilly it wasn't so, and she believed me."

Madame Rayburn stared at me aghast. "You told Lilly it was not so?" she repeated.

I nodded. "I could not find out for two days what was the matter," I explained; "but I got it out of her at last, and I told her that my mother had never written a line to me about her. And she believed me."

"But my dear child," said the nun, "you have told a very grievous lie. What is more, you have borne false witness against your neighbor. When you said to Lilly that your mother had not written that letter, you made her believe that Madame Bouron had lied to her."

"She didn't mind believing that," I observed cheerfully, "and there was nothing else that I could say to make her feel all right."

"But a lie is a lie," protested the nun. "You will have to tell Lilly the truth."

I said nothing, but my silence was not the silence of acquiescence. Madame Rayburn must have recognized this fact, for she took another line of attack. When she spoke next, it was in a low voice and very earnestly. "Listen to me," she said. "Friday is the first of May. You are going to confession on Thursday. You will tell Father O'Harra the whole story just as you have told it to me, and whatever he bids you do, you must do it. Remember that if you go to confession and do not tell this, you will commit the very great sin of sacrilege; and if you do not obey your confessor, you will commit the sin of open disobedience to the Church."

I was more than a little frightened. It seemed to me that for the first time in my life I was confronted by grown-up iniquities to which I had been a stranger. The thought sobered me for two days. On the third I went to confession, and when I had finished with my customary offenses—which, as they seldom varied, were probably as familiar to the priest as they were to me—I told my serious tale. The silence with which it was received bore witness to its seriousness. No question was asked me; I had been too explicit to render questions needful. But after two minutes (which seemed like two hours) of thinking, my confessor said: "A lie is a lie. It must be retracted. Tomorrow you will do one of two things. You will tell your friend the truth, or you will tell Madame Bouron the whole story just as you told it to me. Do you understand?"

"Yes," I said in a faint little voice, no louder than a sigh.

"And you will do as I bid you?"

"Yes," I breathed again.

"Then I will give you absolution, and you may go to Communion. But remember, no later than tomorrow. Believe me, it will get no easier by delay."

Of that I felt tolerably sure, and it was with the courage of desperation that I knocked the next morning at the door of Madame Bouron's office. She gave me a glance of wonderment (I had never before paid her a voluntary call), and without pause or preamble I told my tale, told it with such bald uncompromising verity that it sounded worse than ever. She listened at first in amazement, then in anger. "So Lilly thinks I lied to her," she said at last.

"Yes," I answered.

"And suppose I send for her now and undeceive her."

"You can't do that," I said. "I should tell her again my mother did not write the letter, and she would believe me."

"If you told another such lie, you would be sent from the school."

"If I were sent home, Lilly would believe me. She would believe me all the more."

The anger died out of Madame Bouron's eyes, and a look of bewilderment came into them. I am disposed to think that, despite her wide experience as nun and teacher, she had never before encountered an *idée fixe*, and found out that the pyramids are flexible compared to it. "You know," she said uncertainly, "that sooner or later you will have to do as your mother desires."

I made no answer. The "sooner or later" did not interest me at all. I was living now.

There was another long pause. When Madame Bouron spoke again it was in a grave and low voice. "I wish I had said nothing about your mother's letter," she said. "I thought I could settle matters quickly that way, but I was mistaken, and I must take the consequences of my error. You may go now. I will not speak to Lilly, or to anyone else about this affair."

I did not go. I sat stunned and asking myself if she knew all that her silence would imply. Children seldom give adults much credit for intelligence. "But," I began feebly—

"But me no buts," she interrupted, rising to her feet. "I know what you are going to say; but I have not been the head of a school for years without bearing more than one injustice."

Now when I heard these words sadly spoken something broke up inside of me. It did not break gently, like the dissolving of a cloud; it broke like the bursting of a dam. Sobs shook my lean little body as though they would have torn it apart. Tears blinded me. With difficulty I gasped out three words. "You are good," I said.

Madame Bouron propelled me gently to the door, which I could not see because of my tears. "I wish I could say as much for you," she answered, "but I cannot. You have been very bad. You have been false to your mother, to whom you owe respect and obedience; you have been false to me; and you have been false to God. But you have been true to your friend."

She put me out of the door, and I stood in the corridor facing the clock. I was still shaken by sobs, but my heart was light as a bird. And, believe it or not, the supreme reason for my happiness was not that my difficulties were over, though I was glad of that; and not that Lilly was safe from hurt, though I was glad of that; but that Madame Bouron, whom I had thought bad, had proved herself to be, according to the standards of childhood, as good as gold. My joy was like the joy of the blessed saints in Paradise.

Friends in Adversity

A true, true friend is like a rainbow after a storm.
—AUTHOR UNKNOWN

ROOM WITH A VIEW

BARBARA JEANNE FISHER

*C*omplications from multiple sclerosis had landed me in the hospital—again. I had endured tremors, numbness and muscle spasms, always managing to stay upbeat. But this time was different. This time I had lost my sight. Doctors couldn't tell me when—or even if—I would get it back.

I heard the whir of a wheelchair as the day nurse padded in, her perfume filling the air with the scent of jasmine. "Good morning, Barbara," she said. "I'd like to introduce your room-mate, Joni."

Roommate! I didn't even like my own family seeing me this helpless, much less a complete stranger. I felt a hand clasp mine. "So nice to meet you. I'm looking forward to some company." *Well, I'm not,* I thought. I wanted to draw the curtain between our beds but didn't want her to see me groping around for it. So after the nurse shut the door behind her, I pulled the bedsheet up to my chin, hoping Joni would take the hint and leave me alone.

"Isn't it a lovely day?" she said.

"I wouldn't know," I muttered.

"Can't you feel the warmth of the sunshine?" It was early summer, but the whole world seemed as cold as the fear that gripped me. "It's doing wonders for those beautiful flowers beside your bed. Ruby-red carnations and little white wildflowers with long leafy stems. Someone must really care about you."

I knew how much my husband, my five children, and my

friends loved me. *But they can't help me now,* I thought. Although my illness had made my body weaken, at least before I had been able to see the path ahead of me. Now my days were cloaked in darkness, pierced only by the needles of spinal taps and IV lines. "God, please help me see." The prayer constantly ran through my mind. But my faith was going dark as well.

That evening at dinner I gripped my spoon tightly, hoping Joni was looking the other way. I scooped some porridge-like stuff off my plate and quickly brought it up to my mouth, but I tasted only plastic as the cold mush seeped into my hospital gown.

Instantly, Joni was at my side. "Here, let me help you with that," she said. I flushed with embarrassment, but Joni took my hand in hers and guided a spoonful into my mouth.

"Now the hard part—swallowing it!" she giggled. "It's probably a good thing you don't have to look at the food around here." I smiled.

Despite myself, I started opening up to Joni. Prompted by her questions, I always seemed to end up doing most of the talking. Sharing my life with her, from stories about the kids' antics to the details of my illness, gave me something to focus on instead of my blindness.

After a few days my doctor did another CAT scan and more x-rays and started me on a new medication. "What if I never get my sight back?" I asked Joni.

"Oh, Barb, you will, but even without that, you have so many blessings," she said.

Blessings? Without my vision I could never meet the challenges of living with MS. But Joni wouldn't understand that. She never talked about why she was in the hospital and I didn't want to pry. The doctors didn't spend much time with her. *Must not be that serious,* I thought.

A day or two later, Joe brought all five of our kids to visit. They climbed onto my lap and hugged me just like always, but I worried about my appearance. I had gained some weight because of the medication, and my hair had not been brushed in days.

"I must have looked awful," I told Joni after they'd left. I heard her familiar airy giggle.

"What's so funny?" I asked.

"I wouldn't worry about that—I bet your husband's glad you couldn't see the way he'd dressed the kids. I don't think I've ever seen someone put purple and blue socks with a green striped top." She started describing what each of the kids was wearing, and soon I was laughing so hard my stomach ached. Then she read the cards they'd made for me. "This one has a heart around the 'o' in love. And, oh, this one . . . you have a real artist in the family. I don't think I've ever seen a prettier rainbow."

The next day my doctor gave me another battery of tests. The new drug was having no effect. Joni kept me distracted with her jokes, but I was starting to realize life might never be the same again.

After dinner Joe came to visit alone. He and I talked for the first time about the possibility that I might not regain my sight. "No matter what, you'll always have me and the kids," he said, squeezing my hand tightly. "Always."

When he left I heard Joni stirring. "How lucky you are, Barb," she murmured, "to have so much love in your life."

And then it struck me: there were never many visitors for Joni. Her mother came sometimes and I heard her minister, but that was all. Yet she seemed so content.

How lucky I am to have her, I thought. I buried my head

deep in my pillow. No more thinking only of myself, I decided. I'll ask Joni about her illness and try to return all the kindness she's shown me.

The following morning I woke to the sound of whispers coming from Joni's side. I reached out my hand. The curtain was drawn. Then I recognized the voice of her minister. "May she rest in eternal peace," he said. *But that can't be,* I thought. Any moment I expected to hear Joni's giggle. She couldn't be gone; I had so much to tell her.

I heard the curtain being pulled back. "Joni was ill for a long time. I think she knew this would be her last hospital stay," the day nurse said. "She left a note for you. I'll read it if you like." I nodded. It read:

My friend,

Thank you for making my last days so special! I have found great happiness in our friendship. I pray that you will have your vision back again soon, but just remember: if you can learn to see with your heart you will never really lose your sight.

Remember me with love,

Joni

That night I made out a faint light for the first time in weeks. When I fully recovered my sight, I read my friend's letter over and over. In the years since, I have lost my vision several times, but thanks to Joni I know I will never again lose my way.

A friend is never known till a man has need.
—Author Unknown

Cast All Your Cares
Susan Harris

I came to know the Amish when I was a twenty-two-year-old graduate student doing research for the department of immunology at Duke University. That summer I was assigned to a project in Goshen, Indiana—beautiful farm country with dirt roads and green rolling hills.

My job was to coordinate a tissue-typing study among the area's large Amish population. Because of their close-knit multi-generational communities, the Amish have homogeneous gene pools that are ideal for medical research. I was to seek out families willing to donate blood for scientific studies related to immunology, cancer, allergies, and fertility.

I worried that these peaceful people might feel intruded upon. *I'm a researcher,* I reminded myself. *It's my job to observe them.* But how would they react to a young, independent woman like me racing past their buggies and horses in a rented car?

In Goshen I moved into a Victorian house with a small group of medical researchers. As I made my rounds, trying to gain the trust of the community, one of the first couples I met was Lydian and Amos.

Lydian was a tall, handsome woman with wide-set eyes, tinted glasses, and a winning smile. Just a few years older than I, she already had five children and was expecting a sixth. With two toddlers tugging at her dress, she could still roll out a pie crust, stir a pot of chicken and noodles, and carry on a conversation.

My first task was to interview her mother-in-law. "Mary Schwartz," the woman identified herself. "Schwartz," she said when I asked her maiden name. "Schwartz," she repeated when I asked the question again. Then we both laughed. It was a good introduction to both the small Amish community and their sense of humor.

I went about my business in a scholarly way, only to be captivated by their warmth and wit. When I set up appointments to draw blood, they often suggested breakfast time. And then they smilingly told me that meant 4:00 AM Arriving at a dimly lit farmhouse, I'd grope along the kitchen wall, reflexively feeling for a light switch. Of course, there was none; the Amish use no electricity in their homes. For the family seated around the table, my fumbling in the dark was a real knee-slapper.

Once I asked Lydian's father-in-law, a stocky bearded man just coming in from the fields, if I could draw his blood. "Susan," he boomed, "if the Lord meant for me to give away blood, he would have put a spigot in my arm!" *Oh, dear,* I thought. *What have I done?*

Then he smiled sheepishly and rolled up his sleeve, saying, "I was just pulling your leg."

I realized I couldn't rush from appointment to appointment. I had to allow time to stay for a slice of strawberry-rhubarb pie, a cup of coffee, and a good visit. Then on my way out I would be joined by a new mother, grandmother, and baby for a ride in my car to see relatives on distant farms.

"Why don't you own cars?" I asked Lydian.

"For long trips," she explained, "we'll use public transportation or hire a driver, but for each of us to own our own automobile would surely lead to the breakdown of our community. It would separate us."

As I grew closer to Lydian and Amos, I became impressed by the warm bonds of their family life. Children were everywhere, and Amos was as involved in their upbringing as Lydian. He always had a daughter or son clambering onto his lap. When it came to discipline, voices were rarely raised. The most serious infractions were dealt with a resounding, "Go to the barn!" For Amish children, being sent to their rooms and exempted from chores would be considered a luxury!

I was also touched to see how giving the Amish were. They offered their blood freely. "Why?" I asked Lydian one day.

"It's written in the Bible, 'Thou shalt love thy neighbor as thyself,'" she said. "If donating blood can help others, it's our duty and joy to give."

At summer's end I got married to a fellow I had started dating when I was in school, but the next two summers I returned to Goshen to continue my research. My friendship with Lydian deepened, and as my husband, Stan, and I were eager to start a family, I looked to Lydian for advice on childbirth and nursing.

In 1975 the Duke team presented the results of the Amish study to an international medical conference. Afterward I was besieged by members of the audience. "What a brilliant idea, to use the Amish for research," one man said.

To use them? That's how I had once treated our work, but suddenly I realized how much of the Amish attitude I had absorbed. They had participated in our research out of selfless Christian love. Faith permeated every aspect of their lives. If anyone had used anyone, the Amish had used us to practice their faith.

Back at home I discovered I was pregnant. I took time off from work, and then Stan's bank transferred us to Chicago. At the same time Lydian and Amos moved to an Amish community not far away in Wisconsin, where they helped start a cheese business. Stan offered Amos business advice. And to give them a hand, I began marketing Amish furniture, quilts and toys at regional fairs and exhibitions.

Best of all, each summer we'd spend time at Amos and Lydian's farm. Those were summers filled with the sound of the big teakettle whistling as the children lined up in the kitchen for their Saturday night baths. There were evening devotions in the glow of gaslight and men's laughter in the late-night games of checkers, marbles, and chess. I loved talking to the women over coffee and sweet rolls about marriages, births, weather, our husbands, and our faith.

One day I read a letter Lydian had written to her mother. "Greetings in the Lord from heaven above where all blessings flow!" she wrote in exuberant script. "You are in our prayers." She had such a natural way of expressing her faith.

The years passed. We moved to Connecticut, but we remained close to Amos and Lydian. Then came Stan's stroke.

It was a hot Saturday morning in September. Stan and my father, armed with hammers and wallboard, were converting our garage to a much-needed family room. Our house was bursting at the seams with furniture, books, toys—and our six children. I went out shopping, and when I came home Stan was on the sofa, unable to move his left side.

At the hospital Stan's condition deteriorated. His stroke had been severe. For two weeks he was confined to a hospital bed, uncertain of his future.

Almost at once the letters and cards from the Amish community started coming. Many of the people we barely knew; some we had never met. They had heard about Stan's stroke through Lydian and Amos.

"Greetings and blessings in the name of our Lord!" they wrote. "Cast all your cares upon Him, for He cares for you." Like a heavenly chorus, the messages filled Stan's room.

"You know I've always believed in the healing power of prayer," Stan said one night, after reading the day's mail. "But this is the first time I've ever felt it."

After four months of grueling physical therapy, Stan returned to work. He never regained movement in the toes on his left foot, and his left arm and leg are still weak. But there was a time when doctors doubted that he would ever walk without the aid of a brace and a cane. Stan knows one reason for his healing: the prayers of our Amish friends.

As for our new family room, that project lay unfinished for months, the walboard gathering dust in the garage. Then, one autumn day after the harvest, Amos and Lydian descended on our house with two hired drivers, two rented vans, and fifty-five friends. It was like a real barn raising, what the Amish call a frolic. While we women cooked and cared for the children, the men set to work with hammers, saws, and song. In one week they not only finished our family room but enlarged the living room and added a master bedroom and bath.

That final night of the frolic as I drifted off to sleep, our house bursting with guests, I smiled to myself. The blessings of the Lord had indeed flowed into our lives through our Amish friends.

Adversity not only draws people together
but brings forth that beautiful inward friendship.
—SØREN KIERKEGAARD

THE STRONGEST BOND

LEE NAVES

*D*riving to work one cold January morning, I caught a glimpse of a guy I recognized from high school. He was slumped on the stoop of a seedy liquor store, unshaven, dressed in oily clothes, obviously waiting for the store to open. I shivered. I had a college education and was at the pinnacle of my career as a television reporter. So why, I asked myself, do I so often feel as bad as he looks?

Once in the newsroom I didn't have time to dwell on it. The phone jangled and a mean voice rasped, "How'd you like the biggest story of your life?" The anonymous caller said he was going to poison products in the Bruno chain of grocery stores unless he was paid $300,000. "Tell that on the nightly news, hotshot," he said. Immediately I notified the Bruno corporation.

The FBI tapped my phone so they could trace the call when the extortionist telephoned instructions for the drop. But he hung up before they located him, so they asked me to deliver the $300,000 while they waited out of sight. "Not until I meet Joe Bruno face to face," I said. Mr. Bruno was a rags-to-riches businessman who had founded the grocery chain. No way was I going to put myself on the line for some fat cat unless he could make a pretty good case for himself.

A half hour later a tiny, sixty-nine-year-old man unassumingly made his way into the newsroom. His brown hair was neatly combed away from his high forehead, and his deep-set dark-brown eyes radiated kindness as he peered directly into mine. I got right to it: "Why should I risk my life for you, Mr. Bruno?"

"Well, well," he began, calmly patting his leg on the pauses. "God has always blessed my family, and I trust Him no matter what happens. I wouldn't ask you to risk your life just for me. But I would ask you to consider the innocent people who might be harmed if we don't do something."

I had expected him to hustle me with a sales pitch. I wasn't prepared for his humble appeal. "Think it over," he said, "while I get us some chicken sandwiches."

My mouth dropped open as one of the richest men in town went out to get me a sandwich. How could I turn down a guy like that?

Even though the extortionists got spooked when I arrived at the drop site, the FBI was able to nail them right afterward. Joe Bruno thought I was a hero and arranged for a ceremony at the local FBI headquarters. He gave me a big smile, shook my hand, and handed me an envelope containing a reward check. I didn't feel like a hero and didn't feel right about accepting money for what I had done. I signed the check over to charity.

And that, I thought, was that. When I ran into Joe Bruno a few months later at a building dedication, he told me, "I like what you did with the check. Call me so we can have lunch." I shrugged off the offer, thinking he couldn't be sincere. Not long after, I left the network, thinking the pressures of television broadcasting might have had something to do with my depression.

I became a professor at a local college that had an open-admissions policy. In truth, giving Joe Bruno's check away had made me feel good. I figured teaching disadvantaged kids might also help me feel better about myself. From time to time I received messages that Joe Bruno's lunch invitation was still open, but I always ignored them.

In 1989, seven years after the extortion incident, I read that Joe Bruno would be dedicating a cancer treatment center he had given St. Vincent's Hospital in memory of his family members who had died of cancer. On a whim I decided to go and see if he recognized me. He did, instantly, making a beeline for me and wrapping me in a bear hug. There was no doubting his sincerity.

Over lunch the next week he said, "You look a little down, Lee. Is something the matter?"

I related my frustrations with teaching. Many of my students didn't have the skills to handle my courses; I wasn't getting through to them. "Maybe it's time to quit," I finished.

His answer startled me. "You're a good person, Lee, and those of us who know God have got to help other people. If you don't stick with your students, who else is going to give them a chance?"

I blinked. Here was a man I barely knew, seeing something good in me.

I did give teaching another chance, and Joe Bruno and I set aside a day every few weeks to have lunch. I told him things had picked up at the college.

"Good!" he enthused. "I knew they would. That means you should take another step." With his encouragement I began delivering motivational speeches in public schools.

I have no doubt it was my friendship with Joe Bruno that gave me the confidence to propose to Gayle, a lovely woman I had been seeing for some time. After I told him we had set our wedding date, I said, "Gayle is so self-assured and so incredibly beautiful inside and out. I just hope I'm worthy of her."

He nodded thoughtfully. "Don't worry," he said. "You've found the woman God has planned for you. When I first proposed, I had only fifty dollars to my name. Go get married!"

In June we did. For eighteen months we lived in a storybook marriage.

In December of 1991, I was driving Gayle home from a medical examination when she said flatly, "I could read in their faces that I have cancer. I think it's already spread. If I'm right, I don't want treatments. I want you to go on with your life."

All the breath went out of me. I felt my hands dig into the steering wheel in a death grip. "Gayle," I barely gasped as tears rolled down my face, "what life without you?"

Gayle's doctor confirmed her suspicions—advanced inoperable cancer. As soon as we stumbled out of his office, I found a pay phone and dialed Joe Bruno. I had barely choked out the first sentence when he cut in: "You two meet me at St. Vincent's in an hour for a second opinion. There's a smart young doctor over there."

When we walked into the Joseph S. and Theresa R. Bruno Cancer Center, Joe Bruno was already shaking hands with the staff and patients. Catching sight of us, he grabbed our hands and said, "Let's pray." Oblivious to others in the room, he said, "Lord, we have faith in your will. I've seen miracles in my life, and now I'm praying for one for Gayle."

Over the next few weeks he was present every time Gayle and I visited the hospital for appointments, no matter what the time. After exhaustive testing a specialist said, "We think Gayle is a candidate for a bone marrow transplant." When our insurer balked at the risky $300,000 procedure, Joe Bruno took care of the bill.

In August of 1992 Gayle was put into isolation for a month

after the nearly lethal doses of chemicals were administered to kill the cancer cells. She wanted only three visitors during this period—me, her mother, and Joe Bruno. One day she asked me, "Do you think it would be all right to tell Mr. Bruno I love him?"

"Of course." I smiled, squeezing her hand. "There's nothing he'd rather hear."

Toward the end of her treatments she whispered without a waver of complaint or self-pity, "After today, please, no visitors. Just call. For a while it's going to be only me and God."

As we walked toward the elevator, Mr. Bruno said, "Gayle's giving me the courage to face life and death." Not knowing quite what he meant, I gave him a puzzled nod.

When Gayle's treatments were finished and she was given a clean bill of health, we rejoiced—for two months. By March of 1993 the cancer had returned. Mr. Bruno flew to Lourdes to pray for "Gayle and some other people." Gayle calmly made arrangements for her death. I stood in awe of her . . . and quietly fell apart.

On Tuesday, July 20, 1993, Gayle was taken by ambulance to the hospital, where she was pronounced dead. Joe Bruno was at my side within thirty minutes. He sat down next to me and put a thin hand on mine. He spoke in shallow puffs: "When I lost my wife, all I could do was go to the chapel. And pray every day. Three years passed before I had an answer. God wanted me to marry her sister. Then my brothers died in a plane crash. I can tell you only one thing. Those of us left have to go on. God still has some good for us to do." He paused for a long moment. "It's time to go see Gayle." The thought horrified me, but we both got up stiffly. My eighty-year-old friend limped painfully down the hallway. His hair and eyebrows had turned snow-white, and his forehead seemed to have inched even higher on his crown. I bit my lip and looked at Gayle's still face. She looked so peaceful. Joe Bruno squeezed my hand and prayed, "Lord, accept Gayle's soul and bring your peace to Lee."

Joe Bruno appeared at the funeral home the next morning to help with arrangements. When he spoke at Gayle's funeral, he came not as a VIP but as a friend. Apologizing that "I'm just choked now," he said how much he had loved Gayle and how he had admired her courage. He finished, saying, "She took up her cross and followed Jesus." Walking away from Gayle's grave, Joe Bruno put his arm on my shoulder and said, "Lee, you and me and Gayle have formed the strongest bond in the world. The bond of love."

I couldn't bring myself to go home, much less sleep in the bed I had shared with Gayle, so I checked into a hotel. Joe Bruno called often. After six months had passed he said gently, "You've got to get back out into the world. We still have a lot of good to do." Then he told me about several programs he had heard about to help inner-city youth. I volunteered, and my healing began.

We began meeting for lunch again. "Lee," he said, "I've really missed you." He spoke with such depth of feeling that I found my lip trembling as I looked at the little man with the kind brown eyes. *There's nothing big about this man,* I thought, *except his heart. I can't believe I'm so important to him.* A warm rush of gratitude rippled through my chest, and a sense of peace and well-being flowed through me. Joe Bruno had helped me find enough self-worth to marry the woman of my dreams and now, finally, his respect for me had enabled me to love myself.

"I missed you too," I said.

During the next few months he became frailer. When I asked him about it, he said, "Well, I've got a little problem. I'm going to have some surgery, so I'll have to miss our lunches for a while." We talked on the telephone, but when he didn't have the strength for that either, I kept up with him through his wife.

Joe Bruno died of cancer in January of 1996. He is buried in the same cemetery as Gayle. I miss them terribly, but before I let myself get too melancholy I remember that "we still have a lot of good to do." And out I go. One day I expect to find a fellow, a little down on himself, whom I can help as much as Joe Bruno helped me.

Since there is nothing so well worth having as friends,
never lose a chance to make them.
—FRANCESCO GUICCIARDINI

MY SOLITARY CONFINEMENT

VAN VARNER

*T*here was no indication of trouble when I returned home from Europe last July third. Shep, my Belgian shepherd, was overjoyed at seeing me, running in delirious circles, her tail whacking the living room floor of my apartment on West 81st Street. Though quite tired from the long, uncomfortable flight, I took heart from being at home. After a grateful good-bye to Celeste, a work friend from my preretirement days who had dog-sat while I was away, I took Shep for a walk in the park, then went right to bed. What happened during the night I have no way of knowing, but when I awoke the next morning I was in misery. Pain. My body was racked with it. Terrible pain.

Shep, as always, was waiting for me to get up and attend to her, but simply getting out of bed seemed impossible. "Wait a minute," I gasped. The pain was in my lower back and streaking down my left leg. I'd had my share of aches and pains in life but never anything remotely like this.

At first I wondered if it could be another stroke like the one I'd had two years earlier. *No,* I reasoned, *this is different, more specific.* Could it be because of the straight-backed seat I was marooned in for hours, smack up against a bulkhead, on the cramped transatlantic flight? I didn't know, but why worry about the cause when I had things I must do. I willed myself to get up and get dressed, forcing myself through the pain. What choice do I have? After all, I lived alone.

"All right, Shep," I said, stiffly attaching her leash and heading outside. We had not gone far in the park when I became nauseated. I'd heard the expression "racked with pain," but now I truly knew what it meant. We struggled back to the apartment, Shep casting me a plaintive look as I lurched along the sidewalk. For the next several hours, I lay motionless in bed and tried to think. Only time, I figured, would heal my back. I'd just take it easy for a few days.

I was going to have dinner that night and watch the fireworks on the East River with some old acquaintances. I reached for the telephone gingerly.

"Listen, Daniel," I said when I'd gotten hold of my friend, "if you don't mind, I think I'll pass on the festivities tonight. I'm a little under the weather. Do me a favor and let the others know, please." It seems odd to me now that I didn't mention the trouble I was experiencing. In fact, I was deliberately vague and made an effort to sound as casual as possible. Why bother people with something they could do nothing about?

As the day slowly passed and the pain worsened, I found myself thinking about my mother, who'd died of cancer many years before. Her pain had been severe, yet she did not take medication until the very end. It occurred to me that my mother's suffering was the closest thing I'd seen to the kind of pain I was experiencing now. Had I inherited the tendency to suffer in silence? After all, I'd always believed pain was something you either ignored or battled your way through on your own. Maybe it was my generation. We'd been through so much, the Depression, the war. Keeping a stiff upper lip was second nature.

July Fourth came and went. The sound of Independence Day celebrations that filtered in made me glad I wasn't part of them. I was better off in bed, waiting. All I wanted to be independent from was this incredible pain. I slept and only got up, agonizingly, to care for Shep. By Sunday, July fifth, my condition was no better. Time had not healed me.

On Monday morning I finally called my doctor. After a bruising taxi ride (during which I felt every bump and pothole) and a morning of tests and x-rays, I was told, "You have very likely ruptured a disk in your spinal column, which has irritated your sciatic nerve and caused muscle spasms."

"What about the pain, doctor?" I asked.

"You'll have to wait it out, I'm afraid. If it doesn't stop, we'll see about surgery." He prescribed some pills to lessen the discomfort. I went home and climbed back into bed, suddenly more worried than ever.

That was the beginning of six weeks given over almost entirely to what I deemed The Problem. During that time when pain possessed (and I mean that word) me, I couldn't write or read, couldn't watch television, certainly couldn't be appreciative of the many friends who rallied around me. And they did. Daniel took Shep for her walks, my friend John could be relied on for meals, and Celeste was there for errands when needed. Yet I found myself quietly bristling whenever someone offered a well-intentioned "it will pass" or other words of comfort or encouragement. How could anyone begin to know what I was going through? What could be a more private experience, or a more intensely subjective state, than pain? It was a fog through which people emerged and faded. I was mainly glad to be left alone, at least by humans. Shep, of course, was always within arm's reach.

Still, Celeste was insistent. "Van, I know a physical therapist. She helped me when I hurt my leg last month. Come on, give her a try."

No, for me it was a period of isolation from everybody and everything, a period both good and bad. It was bad, of course, that day after day I was so involved with "me," so focused on my own misery. Some insights, though, did emerge from the experience when I was able to get beyond my own suffering. No longer would I take lightly the words "my aching back," no matter how jokingly they are dispensed. All those who have The Problem have my heartfelt sympathy. Through it all, I grew more aware of others going through the trials of living. That was surely good. Did God inflict this pain on me, or had I done something to bring it on myself? I admit the thought occurred to me. Strangely, as I lay in bed my mind toyed over and over with the same sentence: "Arise, and take up thy bed, and walk." It was from Mark 2:9, yet I didn't think immediately of where it came from. I should have recognized it, for Matthew and Luke and John have similar well-known passages. When it came to me what I was repeating, I grasped its meaning. God didn't want me to suffer. He wanted just the opposite. Jesus' love, the New Testament tells us, can relieve all suffering.

"Oh, yes, help me get well!" I cried out one sleepless night. The sudden outburst woke Shep, who must have wondered what her crazy master was up to. She came over and poked her head at me in a gesture that seemed to say, "All is well. Now let's get some rest."

From that time on, I replaced worry with hope. I stopped pushing away friends who wanted to help and allowed myself to enjoy being in their care. I got in touch with the physical therapist in whom Celeste had such great confidence. Jennifer Nevins became a kind of angel for me. Visiting several times a week, she gently massaged my back and started me on a series of floor exercises, tough going and painful at first, but in time easier, especially when I thought about God's love pulling me through the discomfort. Jennifer also brought me an elastic support band that made me more comfortable when I stood. She showed me how I should lie for hours on an ice pack.

After six weeks I was free of pain. No one is quite sure what caused it, but, by golly, it was there. I am thankful to report that it has not returned, yet I am ready if it does. Pain is a great teacher of humility, a great equalizer, as it were. In a sense it humanizes us by giving us a deeper awareness of the suffering of others through suffering ourselves. I'd always known that love and laughter and friendship brought us closer to one another. I never imagined pain could do the same.

I continue with the exercises just in case, and when I get down on the floor to do them, my friend Shep is, as ever, nearby. "So you're down on my level," she seems to say, her tail thumping, her face ever so pleased.

They travel lightly whom God's grace carries.
—THOMAS À KEMPIS

A FRIEND LIKE JIM

DAVID DOOLEY

*J*im Wells is the kind of fellow you can set your watch by. I should know: We've been best friends for a long time, since our years as long-haul truckers. Though I left trucking, Jim still drives. I always keep him in my prayers when he's out. I know the dangers of the road, so I was quite concerned one Sunday last January when he failed to show up as scheduled after a trip.

I talked with his wife, Cherrie, and reminded her that Jim had said he'd drop by my place when he got back that night. Cherrie said Jim planned to pick up another load in Wellston, Ohio, but had stopped to rest because he was coming down with a cold. He'd called her Saturday from Cincinnati. "But he said he would call me back. He didn't."

"I bet we'll hear from him soon," I said, trying to sound reassuring.

Lord, I hope you have your eye on Jim. Even though I could feel the worry churning in my gut, it felt good to say a prayer. I'd returned to regular churchgoing less than a year before, as a promise to my wife, Susie. I still wasn't used to applying my faith to everyday problems, but I was glad to know I could count on the Lord.

On Monday I called the cargo broker who'd handled Jim's last load. Jim had drawn an advance for his next trip, the broker told me, but had never showed.

Something was definitely wrong. Jim would never miss a load he'd gotten money for. A lone trucker is an easy target for robbery or other crimes. If sudden illness strikes, no one knows something's happened to you. Jim had had some trouble with diabetes lately and he hated to take his medicine. So many things can go wrong on the road. . . .

Cherrie contacted the Ohio state highway patrol and gave them a description of Jim's truck, a bright-red International. They put out a bulletin for him in Cincinnati. Susie, Cherrie, and I prayed that Jim would turn up safe and sound, or that he would call in, cheerful as ever, asking how things were going. Deep down, though, I knew Jim was in trouble. He was far too reliable to leave us in the dark like that. I promised Cherrie that if we didn't hear from Jim soon, or if the police didn't find him, I would go out and search until I did, even if it meant checking every truck stop from Missouri to Cincinnati.

Tuesday passed slowly with no word from Jim. I could hardly concentrate at my job as a mobile-home salesman, even though business was hectic and we were short a person. Finally, on Wednesday morning, I begged my boss for some time off. "Jim's been missing for days," I told him. "I know all the truck stops where he would go."

"Well," he said skeptically, "you do what you have to do, but we could sure use you around here. You really think you'll be able to find your buddy? Why don't you let the police handle it? Probably too late for you to do anything anyway."

Too late?

I'd promised Cherrie I would go out and find Jim, that I'd bring him home. Could I back out on that pledge? When I got in from work that night, Susie could tell something was eating at me.

"Is it about Jim?" she asked.

"The boss says he really needs me, that this is a bad time . . ." I plopped down onto the couch, elbows on my knees, head in my hands. The breath went out of me, long and slow.

"David," Susie said evenly, her eyes catching mine, "you can find a new job any day of the week. A friend like Jim is hard to come by."

That's all she said, but that's all it took. The whole time Jim had been missing, there had been a voice inside me, telling me I had to act, that I couldn't just sit and do nothing if my best friend in the world was in trouble. I realized it was God urging me on. I knew just what He wanted me to do, job or no job: *Find Jim.*

I felt a sense of peace settle down on me—real, true peace I'd felt only once before, when I'd returned to church. That first Sunday I'd felt a powerful sense that I was doing the right thing. This was the first time my new faith was being tested. Was I up to it?

"Toss me the phone, Hon," I said to Susie.

I called Cherrie to let her know I was going out to look for Jim.

"I'll find him, no matter what," I vowed.

The highway was a blur of gray and green on the 400-mile drive to Cincinnati. I couldn't focus on anything but memories of Jim and all the adventures we had had during our years on the road—like meeting up in Bakersfield, California, and going to swap meets, looking for car and truck parts. Or just rendezvousing after a long day of driving for a dinner of chicken-fried steak, potatoes and gravy, buttered biscuits, and some hot blueberry pie, then taking turns on the pay phone to call home. We'd plan our trips together, a two-man convoy. We put in at the same stops, just to keep an eye on each other and to keep from getting too lonely. Loneliness is one of a trucker's biggest foes. It bothered me real bad to think of something happening to Jim while he was out there all alone.

Driving nonstop, I made Cincinnati about 5:30 AM on Thursday, the big, glowing orange globe of a Union 76 truck stop on the horizon. I remembered it was a good place for a quick, hearty breakfast—but a little pricey on fuel. Jim wouldn't have filled up there, but he might have eaten and taken a break.

I pulled off, checking the line of idling trucks for Jim's. No luck. I wasn't hungry, but I grabbed a bite anyway, knowing I'd need my strength. The waitress refilled my coffee cup without my asking. I must have looked like I'd been driving all night.

I hit the road again, searching all the truckers' favorite haunts along Route 32 from Cincinnati to Wellston. I covered about 140 miles. No sign of Jim. I wasn't sure what to do next. I couldn't give up.

Then it struck me: A trucker's wife usually isn't familiar with the territory her husband is traveling. She doesn't know all the little towns he goes through. I used to pick out the biggest nearby city and tell Susie that's where I was. Jim might not have made it to Cincinnati at all. Maybe he was parked in Kentucky, just over the Ohio line. That would have given him an opportunity to get his paperwork in order and catch up on some sleep before picking up his final load. To simplify matters, maybe he just told Cherrie he was already in Cincinnati. It was a long shot, but . . .

I turned around and headed back to Kentucky. About four in the afternoon I crossed the state line and pulled into the first likely station, a Pilot. Cheap fuel, decent food—a good stop for a trucker. Maybe Jim stopped here.

There were several rows of trucks parked and running, glittering in the late-day sun. I got out and walked slowly among them. Even if I didn't find Jim, I could ask some guys if they'd seen him. It was chilly all right, but when I shivered it was not because of the air. There, right in front of me, was a truck identical to Jim's International—red, with gold and black stripes. I checked the license.

I'd found him.

His truck was still running. Truckers usually sleep with the engine idling, so the cab stays a comfortable temperature. With full tanks a truck can run for days. I caught a sharp smell of diesel—almost like burning oil—coming from Jim's rig. That meant the engine had been running for quite some time, not a promising sign.

"Jim?" I called out. No answer. I yelled again. Still no answer. Should I open the door? There was a state police post close by. The best thing to do was to call them, I decided.

The police were there in minutes and a trooper opened the door to Jim's truck carefully, so as not to disturb any evidence of a crime. A second later he called out to me, "I'm sorry, it looks like you're too late . . ."

Too late. I slumped against the side of the cab. My best friend, gone. An ache rose up in me. Why hadn't I come quicker?

"Jim . . . " I moaned in despair, climbing into the cab.

Maybe it was the sound of my voice. All at once Jim sat up, blinking and disoriented, his gray hair mashed to one side. He was clearly in bad shape.

"David," he mumbled, "what the dickens are you doing here?"

"Looking for you, Buddy! You've been missing for five days!"

"Missing? I'm not missing; I'm going to pick up my load . . ." He fell back, too weak to go on. We had to help him sit back up. Out of habit he fumbled for his cap. He never went anywhere without his cap.

Well, it took some convincing while the paramedics got his vitals stabilized, but Jim finally understood the gravity of his situation. Apparently he'd slipped into diabetic shock, most likely induced by the cold syrup he'd taken just before lying down. While he was unconscious he'd developed pneumonia and was slowly drowning in the fluids that had collected in his lungs. With his blood sugar unregulated by medicine, he'd lost nearly twenty pounds.

"He couldn't have made it another day," a paramedic told me. "I'm not even sure how he lasted as long as he did."

I have an idea. Best friends try to look out for each other, especially old truckers. But sometimes we need help. I was tested in my faith, and I learned that when we trust the Lord's urgings, we can never take a wrong turn.

I didn't lose my job. Jim is fine and has promised Cherrie, Susie, and me never, ever to skip his medicine or take something he's unfamiliar with. Thanks to the Lord, a couple of old truckers have a few more good years to enjoy their friendship.

The Bonds of Friendship

Friends are relatives you make for yourself.
—EUSATCHE DESCHAMPS

MY DEIRDRE

LILLIAN MACLEAN

*W*ould you call out Park Street for me?" I asked the trolley conductor, dropping my shiny new nickel into the fare box. "And may I have a transfer, please?"

There were no pockets in my dress, so I tucked my transfer into my sock for the return trip. I took a seat by the window, shivering with excitement. A Saturday afternoon trolley ride to downtown Boston was a great adventure for a ten-year-old in 1938. I loved the hustle and bustle of the city, and I knew my way around very well because Aunt Maudie had taken me there many times. But this time was different.

This time I was going by myself. I'd planned my secret adventure ever since I found the nickel on the street the week before. My aunt would be with her sewing-circle friends all afternoon. *I should venture out on my own,* I thought, *just like Mama had to do.* My mother had been a live-in cook for a doctor's family since my father left us a few years earlier, and I'd lived with my aunt. Maudie was good to me, and Mama visited whenever she could, but I sometimes felt completely alone. I often asked God for a friend, someone I could feel close to every day.

Eagerly I watched as the trolley reached the center of the city. Finally the conductor called, "Park Street!"

"Thank you!" I answered, running for the door. I stepped carefully into the street. Automobiles slowed down to allow the peddlers' carts to pass. Quickly I headed for Summer Street, lined with stores with sparkling window displays of jewelry, glamorous ladies' dresses, and bouquets of flowers. One store offered rows of yummy-looking candy in every color and shape. *Someday,* I thought, *I'll go into the biggest store of all and buy something just for me.*

At the corner of Summer and Washington streets, I spied an ice cream shop. Blue paddles stirred thick cream around in big copper vats. Ice cream was maybe my favorite thing in the whole world, but I didn't dare think of going inside. I wished my mother or Maudie could be with me just to see this wonderful place, and I barely noticed when a woman came up beside me. "Doesn't it look heavenly?" she asked.

"Oh, yes!" I answered. "I've never seen so much ice cream."

The woman smiled. "Would you like to have some with me?"

I couldn't believe my ears. "Yes, thank you," I said, "but I haven't any money."

The woman patted me on the shoulder and opened the door of the shop. "That's all right. I have enough for both of us."

If the ice cream shop had seemed wonderful from the outside, it was pure magic when we entered. The woman chose a table by the window and announced, "We'll have a college ice." She ordered two when the waiter came to our table. "Don't forget the cherries," she said.

The frozen confection arrived in a fluted glass dish. Giant scoops of vanilla ice cream were laced with bits of chocolate and covered with a rich chocolate sauce. On top was a mountain of whipped cream, adorned with a bright-red cherry. Picking up my spoon, I glanced at the woman. It felt like we had been friends for a long time.

We talked as we savored each spoonful. She asked my name, and I told her about my mother and Aunt Maudie.

"My name is Deirdre," she said. "I've come to Boston from my home in Philadelphia for a doctor's appointment."

All too soon our dishes were empty, and we looked sadly at one another. Then Deirdre laughed, and pulled some change from her pocket. She picked through the coins before finding just the ones she wanted. Placing two new quarters on the table, she said, "Take these. Treat your Aunt Maudie to some ice cream."

Deirdre slid the coins across to me with her long, tapered fingers. "How can I thank you?" I asked, slipping the shiny quarters into my sock.

"Tell you what," she said. "Give me your name and address, and I'll write you a letter when I get home. I'd love for you to write me back."

This grown-up wanted letters from me! "I will," I promised. She handed me a piece of paper, and I printed my name and address for her. Then there was a knock at the window. I turned to see a tall woman who looked a lot like Deirdre standing outside the shop.

"That must be my sister," said Deirdre. "She had an appointment, too, and now it's time for us to go home."

Deirdre stood up from the table. "Don't forget to answer my letter," she said. "My address will be on the envelope." She walked to the door then turned back toward me. "Thank you," she said, "for brightening my day."

All the way home on the trolley I thought I'd been living in a dream. Only when I stepped onto our street and felt the coins in my sock did I realize it had really happened. I revealed my secret adventure to Aunt Maudie, and her stern expression softened when I told her about meeting Deirdre. "We're going to be pen pals," I said. Later I shared Deirdre's first letter with my aunt over dishes of ice cream.

Deirdre's letters were beautifully typed, her signature finely penned at the bottom. She was the friend I'd prayed for, and I told her things I couldn't tell anyone else. Deirdre always responded with kindness and caring. For every birthday and every Christmas she included two quarters in my card, a memento of our first meeting. "Buy yourself a treat," she'd say. Then at Christmastime in 1985, no card came. Soon after the holidays a letter arrived from Philadelphia. I knew immediately it wasn't from Deirdre. Someone's handwriting had replaced her familiar typewritten address.

"Dear Lillian," the letter began. It was from Deirdre's sister. "I am very sorry to write to you at this time," she said, "but I know it would be important to my sister that I do so."

The letter informed me that Deirdre had died the week before Christmas and included a startling fact: "Did you know she was almost completely blind?" I learned that all her life Deirdre's vision had been severely limited. "She's always written you on a Braille typewriter," her sister said.

The letter continued: "She enjoyed, more than I can tell you, all your correspondence. You added a great deal of pleasure to her life."

My Deirdre. We had corresponded for forty-seven years. I picked up the box with the 188 quarters I had saved from Deirdre's cards. What proper use could I make of them? Then I remembered the day we met. Someday, I'd thought, I'll go into the biggest store of all and buy something just for me. What did I buy? A gold angel pin that I wear every day so my Deirdre will always be close by.

Best friend, my well-spring in the wilderness!
—GEORGE ELIOT

BETWEEN BEST FRIENDS

GIOIA PASTRE

*J*ayne and I have been best friends since our days at San Marino High School. We were both on drill team. We sang in church choir, we went on trips together, and when we went off to college we chose the same school in northern California.

We didn't see a lot of each other during those four years. We joined different sororities, took different classes, moved in different crowds; but if anything ever went wrong, we would be at each other's side.

I remember she called in tears when she broke up with her boyfriend and the two of us walked around the football field in the pouring rain, singing old high school songs. Or the time I got a low grade on a paper and she and I stayed up until 2:00 AM talking in her dorm room while she convinced me that I wasn't stupid and that the next grade would be better (it was). There wasn't a secret we wouldn't share.

After college we each married, and separately we moved back to our hometown with its peaceful tree-lined streets. Separately, too, we both rejoined the church where we'd sung in choir and had worked in car washes for the youth group. But now we were bouncing infants on our laps, quieting them during worship service, and teaching Sunday school classes of our own.

When Jayne's second child, Brian, turned three, he developed a mysterious growth on the top of his head, right where a baby's soft spot is. Doctors debated whether it was a tumor or a cyst, but no one would know for certain until it was surgically removed.

We took Brian to the hospital. Once again Jayne and I found ourselves together in a crisis. "You drive," Jayne's husband, Ken, said to me, handing me the keys to their car. "I'm too nervous."

At the hospital, after Brian was dressed in a gown, given a shot, and taken to the operating room, the three of us adults sat restlessly in the waiting room with its potted palms and drooping ficus trees. The wait was interminable. We stared blankly at magazines and counted the passing time on the large clock. Every so often a surgical nurse emerged through the swinging doors to alert us to Brian's progress.

Just when I thought the strain was too great we were joined by Den Denning, our pastor. He asked us to pull our chairs together. The aluminum legs scraped on the linoleum floor as we gathered in a circle. "Let us pray," he said.

At any other time I would have been hesitant about praying in public, but the need was so great and Jayne and Ken's fear so palpable, I closed my eyes. While I concentrated on Den's words, I could hear a creaky gift cart go by.

"Lord," he said, "comfort and be with Brian and his parents in this time of need. We ask you to send one of your angels down from heaven. . . . "

At that moment my eyes flickered open and I saw him. He was husky and broad-shouldered, like a football player, and he stood not two feet from me, stretching his diaphanous wings around our circle. I could have reached out and touched his white robe, which flowed to the floor. He was so real. The angel was with us, watching over us.

I shut my eyes again, knowing without a doubt that Brian would be okay. When Ken fell quiet, I opened my eyes to the fluorescent lights of the waiting room. The angel was gone.

Soon a nurse came and told us that the operation was over. The doctors had found no cyst, no tumor. The lump was nothing more than a swelling.

The crisis was over. I wanted to tell Jayne about what I had seen. I had never kept anything from her before, but I was hesitant. I couldn't quite trust myself. How could I explain it? How could I make her believe too?

Nine years passed. I thought of the incident often. Jayne and I took our families on beach trips together. We went to church camp in the mountains with our kids; we went to Mexico with friends. But I never spoke about what I had seen in the hospital.

A couple of months ago, we got together without our husbands or kids. We spent a weekend in the desert at the home of a friend with a few other young mothers from church.

It was almost like high school again. We lounged around a fire, talking about clothes and books and recipes we've always wanted to try. Then the conversation turned serious. When one woman mentioned her guardian angel, I knew I had to bring up the experience I'd had. "I saw an angel once."

Jayne perked up.

It was nine years ago," I said, "in a hospital waiting room—"

"We were praying," Jayne continued, remembering. "He stood beside us and stretched his wings around us."

"And comforted us." We both smiled. It was one more secret we'd shared. The angel had been there—for me and my best friend.

*My friend is the kind of friend who will take care of you
whether or not you want her to.*
—HELEN HOOVEN SANTMYER

TWO FRIENDS AND A STRANGER

SAM MCGARRITY

That morning in 1984 I boarded a plane to Ohio to work on a story for *Guideposts.* Troubled thoughts plagued me. I felt unhappy, mainly with myself.

I'm a writer, I thought dismally, and I haven't even written a book yet. In fact, I was just scraping by.

I envied every married woman who had someone to share life with. "Someone, at least, to share the bills with," I grumbled. I had no husband, and my chances of having a normal family life seemed remote.

Life had never been quite normal since my brother, John, became ill twenty-six years ago. Doctors called him schizophrenic, a hopeless case.

"Nothing I do helps John," I told myself in frustration.

I closed my eyes angrily against the tears. *What kind of life do I have to look forward to?* I wondered.

Little did I know I'd get the answer that day from an eighty-eight-year-old woman—a tiny wisp of a woman. Someone I'd never met, but someone I'll never forget. She was Helen Hooven Santmyer, a scholar, a graduate of Oxford, a writer, a professor of literature, a college dean.

"And now she's famous," I mumbled to myself as I drove from Dayton, where the plane had landed, to a small prairie city called Xenia, Miss Santmyer's hometown.

And to think it all began in a library! I recalled the recent front-page *New York Times* article on Miss Santmyer's fourth book, . . . *And Ladies of the Club,* published in 1982. At first only 1,500 copies had been printed and had ended up over-looked on library shelves.

Two years later, when one of those copies was being returned to the Shaker Heights, Ohio, library, the woman returning it remarked, "This is the best book I've ever read!" Grace Sindell, another library patron, overheard, checked out Miss Santmyer's historical novel (set in a southern Ohio town resembling Xenia), and read it straight through. She then per-suaded her son, Gerald, to read it—Gerald Sindell, the Hollywood producer.

After that, phone calls flew from Los Angeles to New York to Xenia, and the scholarly, taciturn Miss Santmyer awoke one morning in her nursing home bed at Hospitality Home East to discover that she was being offered an option for a TV mini-series. Not only that, her book had also been selected for the Book-of-the-Month Club. Paperback rights to it were being sold for $396,000! Suddenly people all over the country were scrambling to read her book.

Major TV networks and publications swamped the nurs-ing home with calls and reporters. And Xenia jubilantly hung Miss Santmyer's portrait in the town library, established a schol-arship in her name, and affixed a plaque to the front of 113 West Third Street, the family home since 1868. There had not been so much excitement since the tornado of 1974.

Driving through Xenia, I discovered an unimposing, stal-wart little city with squatty brick buildings that had been dark-ened by the years. The town dated from 1803, and a few elegant old homes still stood on tree-shaded streets. A new shopping mall had been built over the tornado ruins, and on Main Street the courthouse tower clock reminded me that it was almost time to meet Miss Santmyer. A granite tablet of the Ten Commandments stood on the courthouse lawn.

In former days pioneers and Indians had traveled through here on the Bullskin Trail. Escaped slaves had passed through on their way to freedom. And this had been home territory for famous Americans like the noble Shawnee chieftain Tecumseh; for Daniel Boone, the educator Horace Mann, and the writer William Dean Howells; for the Wright Brothers. Even for Norman Vincent Peale, who was born ten miles away in Bowersville.

I turned left onto Monroe Street and passed the hospital, where, I was told, ten years ago Miss Santmyer had stood at a window—against nurses' orders—and watched the tornado of 1974 roar down the street. Farther on I pulled into the parking lot of Hospitality Home East.

Miss Santmyer was in her room, lounging in her bed. She held out a thin, blue-veined hand and greeted me pleasantly. We chatted briefly about her book, a picture of small-town life from 1868 to 1932 that hinged on the lives and relationships of the ladies of a literary club, similar to the Xenia Women's Club, to which Miss Santmyer had belonged for fifty-six years.

"Does your book have a message for readers, Miss Santmyer?" I asked.

"I think it has this message: You can have a good life in a simple, undramatic setting. In a town like Waynesboro, the town in the book."

"Or Xenia?"

"Yes, Xenia too," she said.

Miss Santmyer had lived other places—exciting places. She graduated from Wellesley in Boston. She worked at Scribner publishers in New York. She earned another degree at Oxford in England. And then, in 1927, she returned to Xenia.

What kind of life could Xenia hold for a single, well-educated woman like Miss Santmyer? I asked myself.

It was as if I'd spoken aloud. Miss Santmyer proceeded to tell me.

"As soon as I arrived in Xenia, I checked out all the new mysteries from the library. The new librarian, Mildred Sandoe, eyed the pile of books in my arms and offered to give me a lift home."

That was the beginning of almost sixty years of friendship between Miss Santmyer, then thirty-one, and Miss Sandoe, who was twenty-seven. Together they became tourists in Mexico, fisherwomen in Canada, crafts hounds in North Carolina. They shared friends and doctors, and later, in the mid-1950s, after their parents died, they shared the house at 113 West Third Street and a dog named Nicki.

They rented the upstairs apartment to Peggy Shoals, head of the Greene County Historical Society, who would sometimes find "the girls," fondly known as "Santy" and "Sandy," in front of their TV intently watching the Cincinnati Reds or outside pruning the shrubs or preparing for a gathering of the club.

At that moment, Miss Sandoe, who also lived at Hospitality Home East, popped her head in the door. "Just wanted to see how things were going. Are you alright, Santy?" she asked her friend. Miss Sandoe sat with us a while and reminisced about their days in Ohio. Good days, it seemed.

While Miss Santmyer wrote, taught English, and served as dean of women at Cedarville College, Miss Sandoe was driving all over the state of Ohio taking an extensive survey of libraries. She had earned her degree in library science at Simmons

College in Boston. From her survey she wrote a library primer that was used by other states, even other countries, in developing library services.

I could tell Miss Sandoe loved being on the go. "Miss Santmyer and I drove all over the country, sightseeing," she told me. "But I did the driving!"

Miss Santmyer explained: "She claims I went only twenty-five miles per hour, and I think I probably did." She gave a quiet little laugh.

They took short excursions too. On a Sunday afternoon they would follow Route 42 across the Little Miami River and the old Buckeye Trail south to Lebanon, once a Shaker area. They'd order lunch at the Golden Lamb, a historic inn and favorite dining spot—even of nineteenth-century writers Charles Dickens, Mark Twain, and Harriet Beecher Stowe.

Miss Sandoe excused herself after a few minutes. "I have some letters to write," she said. "But you and I must drive down to the Golden Lamb for lunch."

"I'd love to!" I replied.

"You know," Miss Santmyer told me after her friend had left, "Miss Sandoe is answering all of the fan mail. Almost 500 letters have arrived since news went out about the book. Most have been from friends, former students, people we've known through the years."

"Five hundred people!" I echoed. And then, noticing her book on the bedside table, I remarked, "It must have taken a lot of determination and energy to finish . . . *And Ladies of the Club.*" (It was thicker than *Gone with the Wind.*)

"Yes," she replied, "especially toward the end when my publisher said it would have to be cut. I was so sick with emphysema; I was on oxygen and in and out of the hospital. I didn't have the strength. My friend, Miss Sandoe, became involved; it was because she was my very good friend."

Miss Santmyer described how Miss Sandoe painstakingly helped her trim the manuscript—for five years. When Miss Santmyer's health declined to the point that she needed round-the-clock care, Miss Sandoe took the night shift in case Miss Santmyer should roam, find the manuscript, decide she didn't like it, and try to destroy it.

She gave a little laugh. "My friend is the kind of friend who will take care of you whether or not you want her to."

I listened to Miss Sandoe's part in . . . *And Ladies of the Club.* "She not only helped in cutting the manuscript at a time when I was too weak to do it alone," said Miss Santmyer, "but she also has handled all the arrangements for the press. She's written letters, made phone calls, done the organizing, and made appearances when I was not able to. She even mailed the manuscript to the publisher. In eleven boxes!"

After lunch with Miss Sandoe, we stopped by 113 West Third Street and picked some flowers from the garden. They were for Miss Santmyer, of course.

On the plane home, I began to think about the two women I'd just left. Miss Santmyer, eighty-eight, and Miss Sandoe, eighty-four. Both had had outstanding careers. Both had traveled, made friends, influenced young people, felt success. Both had proved Miss Santmyer's point: You can have a good life in a simple, undramatic setting, wherever you happen to be. Even in a nursing home they were still enjoying a full life, enjoying undreamed of success! They had been individuals, pioneers even; and they had loved it and flourished because of it.

And then I thought about myself. I'm a writer too. I don't have a husband or children. And God made me an individual, with my own way of thinking and doing. But the opportunities for me are tremendous. I live in one of the publishing capitals of the world!

As for friends, I've got incredible friends. I've got loads of "Miss Sandoes" in my life. I began to count them. Bob and Emma Baldwin, Jan and Mary Ann and Corona, Jocelyn and Posy and Tom.

These friends have opened their homes to me when I needed a home, they've traveled with me, they've cared for me through sickness, they've shared their feelings and given advice, and they've encouraged me to write. They've been friends to my brother and have celebrated holidays with us.

It was my friend Jan who insisted that I call about the job opening at *Guideposts* almost five years ago. And every opportunity she gets, Corona urges me, "Sam, you've got to write a book about John. It could make a difference. Maybe that's how you can best help John and others who have mental illness."

And I know she's right. That's just one of the challenges waiting for me, but I won't be facing it alone. My "Miss Sandoes" have already made suggestions about outlines and research, word processors, schedules, deadlines!

I'll always be grateful to Miss Santmyer and Miss Sandoe for demonstrating to me that God provides us with challenges. Whoever we are, wherever we are, He blesses us with the support of "Miss Sandoes" to help us meet them.

Thine own friend, and thy father's friend, forsake not.
—PROVERBS 27:10

WHEN FRIENDS FALL OUT

JEANNE HILL

*C*rystal candelabrum. I couldn't imagine how such a beautiful object could come between me and my very best friend. But it was true.

Sheila had seemed to glare at me when I caught her eye during her aunt's funeral. I couldn't understand why and told myself I was seeing the harshness of her grief. Sheila had been raised by her Aunt Flora since her parents died when she was nine.

But later, when I tried to hug Sheila after the burial at the cemetery, she jerked away, her red hair flicking my cheek. "You've got a nerve." Her voice was low, furious.

"Sheila! What are you talking about?" Could I have heard her right? For four months, while she struggled with pre-law courses at a faraway college, I'd been trying to fill in for her with frequent visits to her sick aunt. It had been easy for me to do since I was attending a local nursing school, but it was also a labor of love for her and Aunt Flora.

"You know what I mean," Sheila snapped over her shoulder. "You've had your eye on that candleholder ever since we were kids." She stepped into the black limousine and it pulled away, leaving me feeling as if I'd been slapped.

Unsteadily I walked to my car. Was Sheila really that angry because Aunt Flora had given me the crystal candelabrum? My sweet, generous friend Sheila? It wasn't like her at all! Years ago, when I'd been the new third-grader, the country hick, it was

Sheila who'd befriended me and helped me catch up with the class in the more advanced city school.

Driving home, I thought about the first time I'd seen the beautiful five-branched candlestick and its owner, Aunt Flora. My new friend Sheila had invited me to stop for an afterschool snack at the rambling old Tudor house she shared with her aunt. As we opened the big front door, the sun blazed on the crystal candleholder and I gasped. For there on the entry table where it stood danced a rainbow! And arched across the walls were dozens more of the glistening red, yellow, green, blue, and violet bands!

"It's magic!" I whispered as a tall gray-haired woman came up to us.

"Silly," Sheila laughed gently. "It's just sunlight shining through the crystal."

"It does seem magical," Sheila's Aunt Flora said, stooping down to my height. "Actually, the crystal pendants of the candelabrum are prisms—they make a spectrum of the sun's rays." To prove her point, Aunt Flora turned the delicate crystal pendants first one way, then the other; to my delight rainbows swirled all over the room. "But it still seems magical to you, doesn't it?" She smiled as I nodded my head up and down. "It does to me too," she admitted. From that moment on, Aunt Flora was one of my "special" people.

The candelabrum had never been particularly meaningful to Sheila; but even so, how could she believe that I'd wheedled it out of Aunt Flora?

Inside, I brewed a cup of tea to try to settle my nerves as I tried to think things out. In the strictest sense, the candelabrum should have been part of Aunt Flora's estate and I shouldn't have accepted it. In fact, I'd tried to say as much to her when she'd pressed it on me just two days before she died.

"It belongs here, Aunt Flora," I argued. "I wouldn't feel right taking it."

"Fiddlesticks!" There was a tremor in her usually crisp voice. "I'm leaving everything to Sheila except that candle-holder. She doesn't care about it and you do." She laid her thin hand over mine. "You can't imagine what it's meant to me, your coming here two and three times a week to read my Bible to me. You're a precious friend to me and Sheila. You must take it."

At that point, Mrs. Wagner asked me to help her with something in another room. When we were alone, she urged me not to upset Aunt Flora any further by refusing the gift. "Her heart can't take the slightest agitation," she warned me.

Now, I set down my teacup with a decisive click. When Sheila knew that, everything would be fine. Tonight I'd go to her house and explain.

But I didn't get the chance. When Sheila answered my ring, she gave me a cold stare. "Please. Go away," she said curtly. As I hesitated, she closed the door.

Two miserable weeks went by before I figured out what to do. I wrapped the candelabrum carefully and sent it to Sheila. I included a note explaining why I'd accepted it.

The next afternoon, while I was cooking my dinner, the package came back with an icy unsigned message: "I'm sure you know I can't keep this because it was recorded on a personal-gift list Aunt Flora sent to her accountant."

As I stared at the note, the hurt I'd been feeling shriveled like paper in a roaring fire. This was no friend of mine. This shrewish, selfish person wasn't the Sheila I'd known. Trembling with outrage, I went to the phone and dialed her number.

"Hello," said the familiar voice.

"Sheila, you've treated me like a dog and you've killed our friendship. I'll never forgive you."

Click. She hung up.

"Good," I told myself as I banged around the kitchen. But I couldn't eat a bite of the food I'd prepared. I sat there into the evening, the anger draining away, wondering what to do. I thought about Aunt Flora and how she'd grieve about the shattered friendship. I thought of her worn hand resting in mine, her serene face as I'd read to her from the Bible. Where had we left off? Was it Ephesians?

I got out my Bible and turned to Paul's letter to the church at Ephesus. I read for about twenty minutes before I came to verses thirty-one and thirty-two of chapter four. "Let all bitterness and wrath and anger and clamor and slander be put away from you, with all malice, and be kind to one another, tenderhearted, forgiving one another, as God in Christ forgave you." (RSV) I stopped reading. *How Lord?* I pondered that question until bedtime.

Then, to make matters worse, something terrible happened on my way to work. I was driving in rush-hour traffic when the speckled hound from the landfill—I called it "dump dog"—zigzagged right in front of me! I couldn't swerve in any direction without hitting a car. I saw the terror-filled eyes of the dog and felt a thud under my front tire! Brakes squealed and horns honked as the yelping dog dragged himself off the road.

I maneuvered to the outside lane, parked on the shoulder, grabbed a small picnic blanket from my trunk, and ran back to the whimpering dog. When I lifted him, I knew the pain would very likely make him try to bite me. Protecting my hands with a fold of blanket over them, I spread the rest of the cover over and under the dog's hindquarters. His eyes were glazed with pain.

As I lifted him into my arms the blanket slipped off one hand. His head moved. Frantically I braced, expecting his sharp teeth to sink into my wrist. But instead, amazingly, I felt a warm, rough tongue. Even though I was hurting him, the dog was licking my hand.

After I'd driven the dog to the nearest animal hospital and been assured he would live, I made up my mind about two things: the "dump dog" was coming home to live with me. And if a dog could forgive such pain from a stranger, I could certainly do as much for a friend.

And now I knew how.

A lowly "dump dog" showed me that God's way to forgive is to return pain with love, to fill your heart so full of love for the person you're angry with that there's no room left for resentment.

On the way to Aunt Flora's house to see Sheila, I reminded myself that she would probably close me out. But I also knew that no matter what she might say, I would react with love.

Walking up the porch steps, I filled my mind with all the good memories we shared. As soon as Sheila opened the door, I began to talk, "Sheila, I care about you. I finally understand how hard it must be for you to lose Aunt Flora, your very last relative. I'm sorry I haven't done a good job of showing you my love, and I just ask that you give me another chance to be the friend I want to be."

Sheila's hand stopped in the motion of shutting the door, and she dropped her eyes from my face. I touched her arm lightly to make her look up and raced on: "So, please, Sheila, don't turn me away."

The rigidness in her body seemed to begin to relax, and she leaned tiredly against the door jamb. "I've come to ask your forgiveness, Sheila," I said in a low, urgent voice. "Forgive me for being defensive when I should have been loving and for reacting to you with anger when I should have been understanding."

We were both silent. Then Sheila sighed deeply. "You don't owe me an apology," she said. "There are some things you need to know." Her voice caught. "Some things that are hard for me to tell you. Come on inside."

She swung the door wide and I stepped into the familiar entry. "Aunt Flora's minister has been counseling me, trying to help me cope with the awful guilt I feel about not being here when Auntie needed me. Her doctor told me she might linger for over a year—that he'd let me know in plenty of time to be with her at the end. But that's not how it happened. It was so sudden. I came as soon as he called, but she never regained consciousness to know I was here."

"I didn't know that! Oh Sheila, I'm so sorry."

She shook her head. "You may not feel so sympathetic when you hear the rest. Only yesterday the minister made me see that I resent you because you were here when I wasn't. When Aunt Flora gave you the candelabrum, it showed how much you and your visits meant to her, and that multiplied my guilt.

"Jeanne, I'm so ashamed, I'm really thankful you were with Auntie! I'm the one who should apologize! But I'm not sure I'd have had the nerve unless you made the first move. Can you ever forgive me?"

"I already have, Sheila," I said. It was true. My forgiveness, my peace of mind, had nothing to do with Sheila's apology. It had come earlier, before I knew about the minister's insights or how Sheila would respond to me. It had come when I'd learned to love her God's way, with total acceptance.

I looked at Sheila's solemn face and smiled. And we fell into each other's arms.

Real unselfishness consists in sharing the interests of others.
—GEORGE SANTAYANA

THE TRUEST OF FRIENDS

NANCY SULLIVAN GENG

S pulled the pink envelope from our mailbox just as my daughter was coming home from school. It looked like a birthday party invitation. "SARAH" was carefully printed in bold, black letters. When Sarah stepped off the bus, I tucked the envelope into her hand. "It's . . . it's . . . for me," she stuttered, delighted.

In the unseasonably warm February sun we sat down on the front porch. As I helped her open the envelope, I wondered who had sent it. Maybe Emily or perhaps Michael, pals from her special-education class.

"It's . . . it's . . . from Maranda!" Sarah said, pointing to the front of the card. There, framed with hearts, was a photo of a girl I had never seen before. She had beautiful long hair, a dimpled grin, and warm, smiling eyes. "Maranda is eight years old," the caption read. "Come and celebrate on Valentine's Day."

Glancing at the picture, I felt uneasy. Clearly, Maranda was not handicapped. Sarah, on the other hand, had Down's syndrome and was developmentally delayed in all areas. At age nine she still functioned on a preschool level. Her disability was obvious, marked with thick-lensed glasses, a hearing aid, and stuttering.

A happy child, she had many friends who used wheelchairs and braces and walkers. But this was the first time she had been invited to the home of a nondisabled child. "How did you meet Maranda?" I asked.

"At . . . at . . . school. We eat lunch together every . . . every day."

Even though Sarah was in special education, she socialized with other second graders during gym, lunch, and homeroom. I had always hoped she would make friends outside her program. Why, then, did I feel apprehensive?

Because I'm her mother, I thought. I loved Sarah. I wanted and prayed that she would have the best. I also knew a friendship with Sarah called for extra sensitivity, tolerance, and understanding. Was the child in the photo capable of that?

Valentine's Day came. Sarah dressed in her favorite pink lace dress and white patent leather shoes. As we drove to Maranda's party, she sat next to me in the front seat, clutching the Barbie doll she had wrapped with Winnie-the-Pooh paper and masking tape. "I . . . I'm so excited," she said.

I smiled, but deep inside I felt hesitant. There would be other children at the party. Would they tease Sarah? Would Maranda be embarrassed in front of her other friends? *Please, Lord,* I prayed, *don't let Sarah get hurt.*

I pulled into the driveway of a house decorated with silver heart-shaped balloons. Waiting at the front door was a little girl in a red sweater trimmed with ribboned hearts. It was Maranda. "Sarah's here!" she called. Racing to our car, she welcomed my daughter with a wraparound hug. Soon seven giggling girls followed Maranda's lead, welcoming Sarah with smiles.

"Bye, Mom," Sarah said, waving as she and the others ran laughing into the house. Maranda's mother, Mary, greeted me at my rolled-down car window.

"Thanks for bringing Sarah," she said. "Maranda is so excited Sarah could come to her party." Mary went on to explain that her daughter was an only child and that Maranda and Sarah had become special friends at school. "Maranda talks about her all the time," she said.

I drove away, amazed. Still, I couldn't get over my uneasiness. Could this friendship ever be equal? Maranda would need to learn the language of Sarah's speech. She would need patience when Sarah struggled with certain tasks. That was a lot to ask of an eight-year-old.

As the months passed I watched the girls' friendship grow. They spent many hours together in our home. Fixing dinner in the kitchen, I heard giggles fill the family room as they twirled around an old recliner or watched *The Lion King*. Other times they dressed up in my old hats and outdated blouses, pretending to be famous singers. Soon the months turned to years.

One afternoon in late autumn, 1995, I watched the two of them sitting next to each other at our kitchen table. Sarah held a pencil; Maranda had a tablet of paper.

Maranda called out each letter as she guided Sarah's hand: "S-A-R-A-H." Though some of the letters had been printed backward or upside down, Maranda praised Sarah's effort. "Great job," she said, applauding.

At Christmastime the girls exchanged gifts. Sarah gave Maranda a photograph of herself, a framed first-communion picture. "You look beautiful," Maranda said as she admired Sarah's white ruffled dress and long lace veil. In return, Maranda gave Sarah a gray-flannel elephant trimmed with an "I love you" tag. It quickly became Sarah's favorite stuffed animal, and she slept with it every night.

A few weeks into the new year, Sarah came home from school looking downcast. "M-Maranda is . . . is sick," she said. I thought maybe she had caught the bug circulating at school. Minutes later, however, Sarah's special-education teacher called.

Maranda was in the hospital. She had sustained a seizure at school and had been diagnosed with a brain tumor. Surgeons had performed a risky operation, which had left Maranda paralyzed on one side with impaired speech and vision. The biopsy results weren't back yet.

"Can we visit her?" I asked. I knew Sarah would want to see her friend.

"Maranda is very despondent and not up to seeing anybody," the teacher told me. "Her parents are requesting cards rather than visits."

"We'll keep her in our prayers," I promised.

That night Sarah knelt beside her bed, clutching her stuffed elephant. "Please ma . . . ma . . . make Maranda better," she prayed. Night after night she implored God to heal her friend. Then one night in early February, Sarah stopped abruptly in the middle of her prayer. She nudged me.

"Let's ma . . . ma . . . make a valentine for Ma . . . Maranda."

The next day we sat together at the kitchen table as I helped Sarah write Maranda's name on a large sheet of pink-and-white construction paper. She decorated each letter with stickers and glittery Magic Markers. She drew a large heart around the name, then glued candy hearts with phrases like "friends forever" and "be mine." In similar fashion she added four more pages. Just before we slid the card into a large envelope, Sarah asked, "How . . . how . . . how do I spell love?" I called out the letters as she painstakingly printed "LOVE," the letters crooked and out of place, followed by her name.

Two weeks passed. We heard that Maranda had additional surgery. On Valentine's Day I got a phone call from her mother. "Maranda's home," she said, "and wants to see Sarah."

"Home?" I asked with surprise.

"Maranda's tumor was benign. We're hoping for a full recovery."

As we discussed Maranda's prognosis, she relayed how thankful she was for Sarah and her card. "Maranda was very depressed. She had stacks of letters, cards, and gifts but wouldn't open any of them. Then one morning Sarah's homemade card arrived. We opened it and Maranda burst into a huge smile. She hugged it and wouldn't put it down." Mary's voice was choked with emotion. "It was an answer to prayer."

I realized then that Sarah and Maranda were the truest of friends. Their bond was defined not by intellect or health or handicap, but by love, unconditionally given and received. They had overcome disability with laughter and support. Their friendship had always been equal.

Today both girls are doing well. Maranda is almost twelve and Sarah is going on thirteen. With the help of intensive therapy, Maranda's neurological functions returned to normal, and Sarah's speech has improved immensely. She can even read some. Though we've moved to a different neighborhood, the girls still keep in touch. Recently Maranda came to sleep over.

As the girls sat at our kitchen table, they talked about Maranda's newly pierced ears and Sarah's "secret" boyfriend from her special-ed class. Then in the middle of their conversation, Sarah opened a kitchen drawer and pulled out a tablet and pencil.

"S-A-R-A-H," Maranda called out, just like old times. As Sarah printed her name without any help, Maranda looked on and clapped.

"Great job, Sarah!" she said.

I took a peek at my daughter's masterpiece. Her name had been written perfectly.

You can always tell a real friend: when you've made a fool of yourself, he doesn't feel you've done a permanent job.
—LAURENCE J. PETER

MY HUNDRED FRIENDS

BEN HECHT

*W*hat fun living would be if all our friendships survived! If all the chums and partners we had still clamored to see us and we them! How rich our existence would be were it full of that fine cast of characters with whom we played the many scenes of our lives.

But we must grow old on an emptying stage and in a corner of it, usually. And if anybody speaks our name we are likely not to know theirs. It is a lucky man who after fifty-five can call anyone "old friend."

Our friends vanish with the events that produce them. I look back on a hundred friends, each of them a fellow who once seemed a vital part of my day and is no part of it now.

This is not as depressing as it sounds. I, for one, have never regretted vanished friendships. They are like money happily spent.

I know men who make a career of not permitting friendships to lapse. They keep telephoning, writing, getting together. But when I look closely at the continued friendships of such men, I note that it is with "important" people the friendship is kept going. This is the thing that keeps celebrities knowing one another longer than people of no renown. Long after their intimacies have ended, celebrities continue to pool their fame. Being together is no longer friendship for them but something almost as important—good publicity.

The cafes of New York and Hollywood are filled nightly with a comradeship more for the camera than the soul.

Obviously when I think of how pleasant life would be if our friendships survived, I am not thinking of my old friends alone but of my own vanished enthusiasms. It is in their air that my old friends breathed and it is for those heady atmospheres I mourn.

I can see now that any time I loved anything, friends bloomed magically around the thing I loved. If it was only walking or playing cards, friends appeared to share and increase my pleasure. They stepped out of limbo and became my fellow dreamers. And there were times when it was not I and my activities that lured partisans. There were times when I loved myself.

Out of many friendships I have learned a few unvarying qualities. Most important is the quality of impermanence. Friendship is the thinnest of cements. A change of job or a move to a different street can break the pleasantest of friendships. Marriage can put an end to a dozen of them without a word being spoken. Success requires us to change our friends, as does failure. Persistent calamity is also fatal.

Loyalty and sacrifice, if called on too much, destroy a friendship quickly. It is possible to love a woman who has only troubles to give us. But a friend with similar impediments ceases to be an equal and thus, automatically ceases to be a friend.

I have noted that the best and closest friends are those who seldom call on each other for help. In fact, such is almost the finest definition of a friend—a person who does not need us but who is able to enjoy us.

I have seldom suffered over the troubles of a friend. . . . And he is seldom serious in telling me of his misfortunes. He makes anecdotes out of them, postures comically in their midst and tries to entertain me with them. This is one of the chief values of my friendship, as it is of his. We enable each other to play the strong man superior to his fate. Given a friend to listen, my own disasters change color. I win victories while relating them. Not only have I a friend "on my side" who will believe my version of the battle—and permit me to seem a victor in my communiqués—but I have actually a victory in me. I am able to show my friend my untouched side. My secret superiority to bad events becomes stronger when I can speak and have a friend believe in it.

Another asset a friend has to offer is the fact that he is a soothing fellow—always half a bore. There are no mysteries to him. He may think he has secret characteristics that are hidden from me. But this is literally impossible. . . . An enemy is a sealed arsenal of vices, a friend is an open clinic.

In fact, I have thought more downright scandal about friends than about an enemy. The fact that I can see his failings so plainly is one of the things that make him my friend. . . . I am daily aware that he brags, forgets, is blind as a goat toward his own lapses, and I feel often that only a miracle can save him from disintegration.

Yet my friend's faults never alienate me, for I am, somehow, never their victim. In a mysterious way his friendship keeps him from directing his faults at me. He will point them at his wife . . . and his enemies. That is why his faults are comic to me. He is harlequin and never horror.

There are many other qualities to friendship, such as the absence of competitiveness. A friend is a rival whom I wish well, whose success does not irk me but adds almost as much to my importance as to his. There is also the quality of love, an odd, unsensual love, a love without greed or possessiveness, the sort of love one has for an infant or a book or life itself.

Such brotherhoods, dead and alive, hold in them most of my history. While writing this book I have looked forward to telling the stories of my friends, not alone because I have desired to meet them again but because I hoped to recapture the happy things in my life that produced them.

Memories
of Friends

*There is no possession more valuable
than a good and faithful friend.*
—SOCRATES

WALLY

ANDY ROONEY

I see a lot of my friend Wally in the summer. Wally is the best old friend I have ever had. I haven't known him for long but he's eighty-two. That's an old friend. My relationship with most people I've known who were that age has been distant. I felt separated from them. I've loved some, admired many, and felt sorry for quite a few older people; but I never had a pal eighty years old until I met Wally.

Wally and his wife have a place in the little village where we spend much of our time in the summer. Our house is on top of the hill about a mile out of town. What Wally and I have in common, in addition to that indefinable sense of understanding one another that friends have, is an interest in woodworking. We travel around the countryside together looking for good pieces of cherry or walnut in some of the little sawmills, and we swap tools and exchange problems. Wally's idea of a good time is to drive into the city and buy a new tool. That's my idea of a good time too. Each of us has more wood and more tools than we know what to do with.

Wally's real name is Wellington, and he has the stature to handle that kind of a name, although no one ever calls him by it. Wally is six-foot-five, a giant of a man and still strong. When I go down to his workshop with a problem, he'll dig out one of his cabinetmaker's books that explains what to do in detail. He goes to the book more often than I do. He'll come out of his workshop and put the book on top of his car parked in the driveway at the side of the house and start looking for the answer to my problem. He points to some page in the book. The problem is, he's eight inches taller than I am so my eyes are only on a level with the top of his car. He's looking down on the book. Last week, for instance, I was trying to find out how to bend a piece of oak by steaming it, and Wally read to me how to do it from his book on top of the car.

Later in the day I came by again, and Wally was worried because he couldn't remember where he'd put the cabinetmaking book we'd been looking at. He was afraid he might have absentmindedly left it on top of the car and that his wife had driven off with it up there. Wally's very aware of his age, and he thinks he's more absentminded and forgetful than he used to be. I don't know, of course, but I suspect he's always been about the way he is now. Forgetfulness seems to come very naturally to him.

"There are three things bad about getting old," he says. "One, you can't remember anything . . . and I forget the other two." He laughs. Wally likes old jokes.

Early in the summer when we first came here, I went down to greet Wally. We talked about our winters and then he said, "Hey, come in here a minute."

We went to his crowded workshop, and he pointed to a pile of pieces of cherry on his workbench. There were four carefully turned and fluted legs, several small pieces that had been dovetailed or rabbited, and one wide board that looked like the top of something.

"Look at this stuff," Wally said. "I did this at the end of last summer and left it here, and now I can't remember what the hell I was making."

Wally has better tools than I have, but his workshop is just as much of a mess. He says he waits until the sawdust reaches his knees before he cleans it out. Last week I loaded up my station wagon with scraps of wood and two barrels of sawdust to take to the dump. Wally went with me, but when we got there the people in the little office at the entrance to the dump said I had to have a sticker on my car to prove we were residents.

I filled in a form, but I had to go outside to look at my license plate number. "Hey, Eddie," I heard one of the men say to another. "How about that. He don't even know his license plate number."

Wally decided he ought to get a dump sticker, too, so he came back into the office with me. He started filling out the form, and when he came to the license plate question he looked up at the dump man and said, "I don't know my license plate number." The man shook his head and gave a knowing look at Eddie. To him it was evidence that we were two dumb city slickers, neither of whom knew his license number. To me it helped explain why Wally and I are such good friends.

When Wally was known as Wellington, he was vice-president of a very big corporation. He must have been good at his work to have been so successful but I suspect Wally never did anything better in his life than he does being eighty-two years old.

Friendship is a sheltering tree.
—SAMUEL TAYLOR COLERIDGE

UNEXPECTED FRIEND

SHARON ROBERTSON

*O*ur classroom bustled with the usual uproar of rattling lunch boxes and shouting fifth graders. Jack Jayson had Bud Munion pinned in the corner.

Suddenly, at the sound of approaching footsteps, we ran for our desks, leaving Bud on the floor. We transformed ourselves into perfect little ladies and gentlemen, hands folded, feet planted. The door swung open; everyone rose in unison and said, "Good morning, Sister Miriam." The girls curtsied; the boys bowed.

"Good morning, class," she said. "May God spare us all for a wise and good purpose. Bud, get off the floor!" Bud staggered to his feet.

"Class, we have a new student today. She comes all the way from India. Say good morning to Santos Ramir!"

We looked at the girl in the doorway. Her dark eyes were as big as saucers; her hair was thick and black. Her uniform was two sizes too large, and her legs were so skinny that her navy-blue knee socks had slid down, crumpling around her ankles.

"Who will be Santos's buddy this week?" Sister Miriam asked. I cringed. A new student was bad enough, but to be friends with a foreigner was too much. "Sharon, will you?"

I felt the blood drain from my face. My mind scrambled for an excuse. I swallowed hard and replied, "Yes, Sister."

Santos took the seat next to me. She smiled at me, then

grabbed my hand, swinging it back and forth for all to see. My stomach turned.

When the lunch bell rang, I led Santos to the playground, where I hoped no one would spot us eating together. I opened my lunch box: a cream-cheese-and-jelly sandwich, an apple, and a Devil Dog. Santos opened hers: a sandwich wrapped in greasy waxed paper. She peeled the paper away to reveal yellow meat with a ferocious odor.

"What is that?" I asked in disgust.

"Curried beef on pita. What is that?" she asked.

"Cream cheese and jelly."

"Yuck!"

"What do you mean? This is American. This is good!"

"Mine is good too!" Santos ripped her sandwich in two, giving me half. In the name of good manners, I gave her half of mine.

Other classmates joined us in the playground. My friend Suzette said, "Sister Miriam's birthday is in two weeks, and my mother told me that someone else's mother should bake a cake this year. Can your mother do it?"

Before I could answer, Santos blurted out, "My mother will!"

Suzette looked at her skeptically. "Your mother can bake?"

"She bakes me cakes all the time."

"Well, okay." Just then she sniffed at Santos's sandwich. "What's that smell?"

Meanwhile, Jack Jayson came over, screaming: "Hey, Santos Claus." Then he took a whiff of her lunch. He jumped back, holding his nose and chanting, "Santos Claus has dirty paws." Before we knew it, we were surrounded by kids repeating the chant. I yelled for them to leave Santos alone, but it was out of control. There was nothing left to do but retreat.

Back in the classroom, Santos was crying so hard that she had soaked the collar of her uniform. Sister Miriam knelt down to comfort her and gave her a piece of licorice from her own private stock. Sister Miriam loved licorice above all things.

Drying her eyes and chewing her licorice, Santos thanked me for sticking up for her. "You're my best friend," she said.

I was so stunned I could only reply, "Okay."

Sister Miriam sent Santos to the bathroom to wash up, then slipped me some licorice too. "I'm proud of you, Sharon," she said, "for defending Santos. Remember what Jesus said: *'Inasmuch as ye have done it unto one of the least of these my brethren, ye have done it unto me.'"*

I looked at my shoes, embarrassed and ashamed. I hadn't defended Santos because I wanted to. I did it because of Sister Miriam.

Much to my surprise, Santos and I quickly became friends. She came over to my house and played with my dolls. I went to her house and played with Indian dolls that her grandmother had made by hand. As a token of our friendship, her grandmother gave me my own Indian dolls. So I gave Santos some of my Barbies.

But back at school I kept my distance. With my halfhearted protection, it had been a hard two weeks for Santos. Her classmates alternated between ignoring her and taunting her. "Just wait until my mother brings Sister Miriam's cake," she kept telling me. "Then everyone will see." But it was hard for me to see how a cake would make any difference.

Finally the big day came—Sister Miriam's birthday. Santos watched the clock anxiously. All she could talk about that morning was the cake. None of us ate any lunch so we would have room for big pieces.

In the afternoon Santos's mother entered the classroom with a large box that she set on the desk. As we sang "Happy Birthday," Sister Miriam removed the hankie from her sleeve and dabbed her eyes. Santos beamed with pride when her mother stepped back, bowed to Sister Miriam, and left.

It was time for the unveiling. I could hear my stomach growl. Slowly, triumphantly, Santos took the contents from the box.

We looked at it, stunned. The cake was black. A black cake?

"It's as black as my boot!" Jack Jayson exclaimed. The class broke out in side-splitting howls. I tried to keep my composure, but I could feel the laughter coming up from my belly. How could Santos do something so dumb?

Sister Miriam raised her voice: "That is enough!" Santos's head hung low; her tears splashed on the floor. I knew I had to help.

Nervously, guiltily, I poked a finger in the icing and tasted it. Licorice! I stamped my foot and bellowed, "It's licorice, you idiots! Sister Miriam's favorite." A silence fell over the class.

"Licorice," Jack finally said. "That was a great idea, Santos."

"Great idea," others murmured.

"Who wants a slice?" Sister Miriam asked.

"I do," "I do," "I do," came the responses. Santos smiled; suddenly she had many friends, but I was glad I had been there first. It was the best thing I had ever done. I felt wonderful. And when I overheard Suzette invite Santos to her house after school, I was just a tiny bit jealous.

When a friend speaks to me, whatever he says is interesting.
—JEAN RENOIR

A CUP OF CHRISTMAS TEA

TOM HEGG

*A*t first I did not think I could do it. In fact, when I was asked to write and perform something for my church's 125th anniversary in December 1981, I struggled to come up with some monumental idea.

As a teacher and actor, I spent a lot of time wondering what sort of universal statement I could make about Christmas. Finally, one night after my son was tucked in bed and my wife was asleep, I sat down and started to write. But what came out wasn't intellectual or panoramic or grand. It was a poem, simple and straightforward.

The cards were in the mail;
All the gifts beneath the tree . . .

It was past midnight, but still I wrote and the words came flowing out.

Something still was nagging me
and would not go away . . .

The poem went on to tell of a letter from an infirm and elderly great-aunt who hopes her nephew can make time to drop by for a cup of Christmas tea. The narrator forces himself to fit in a visit that he fears will be depressing, only to find a house lovingly filled with childhood memories and a great-aunt whose eyes still sparkle and words still encourage.

Her body halved and nearly spent,
but my great-aunt was whole.

I saw a Christmas miracle,
the triumph of a soul.

I finished the poem three days later and called it "A Cup of Christmas Tea"; and when I got up to read it at the church, I must admit my knees were shaky. So was my grip on cadence and phrasing. When I stopped reading, there was silence. I guessed I'd been wrong to present my little verse on such an important occasion.

Then the applause started and didn't stop. The audience stood up to clap, some people wiped their tears. I was as astonished as anybody.

In the days that followed, people told me that because of my poem, they, too, had visited elderly relatives or friends who were ill or homebound. People asked again and again where to get the book. "But I don't have one," I explained.

Would a book be possible? If so, I knew I'd need an illustrator. Where could I find one?

"Warren Hanson is the best in town," I was told. "He's got his own commercial art firm and some big advertising clients. He's in demand, but you could give him a try."

For years I'd been on stage with the Tyrone Guthrie Theater and had performed complicated speeches in front of a lot of people. But never have I been as tongue-tied as I was when Warren Hanson answered my phone call.

"I've, ah, got this little poem," I said. "I don't have a publisher, and I don't have any money. Would you be interested in doing the illustrations?"

"I'm sorry," Warren said politely. "I just don't have the time."

I don't know what gave me the nerve. I started to read the poem aloud, waiting for him to cut me off at any moment.

"Come in! Come in!" She laughed the words.
She took me by the hand,
And all my fears dissolved away,
As if by her command.

When he didn't interrupt, I kept going. And when I had finished, I heard him take a deep breath. "I just visited my aunt in southern Minnesota," he said. "And I had the same sort of experience. Count me in."

Warren was convinced that watercolors in pastels would be right for the gentle spirit of the book. There was only one problem: "I've never worked in watercolors before," he told me. Wouldn't it take even more time from his busy schedule to learn a new technique? "That's okay," he said. "I really want to do it."

Even more important, we agreed that the artwork would not show people but houses, trees, teacups, and ornaments instead. We wanted readers to envision themselves making that visit, to see their own loved ones as they turned the pages.

I presented our book proposal to some publishers in New York City but was told that poems didn't sell and holiday books were too seasonal. Besides, Warren and I weren't known in the publishing world. Nobody wanted to bother with us.

My spirits were particularly low on the day I went to my mailbox—and found a letter from actress Helen Hayes! I'd always greatly admired her, and impulsively I had sent her a copy of my manuscript. "Your Christmas poem is a treasure," she wrote. "It brought tears of joy to my eyes."

That note of encouragement gave me the energy to proceed. Using a $10,000 loan from my parents, I published 5,000 copies of the book myself. When they sold out in area bookstores, Warren and I were overjoyed. But because we didn't know anything about marketing and distribution, we'd barely broken even. How could we continue?

It was then I got a phone call from a Minneapolis businessman named Ned Waldman. He was a publisher and an owner of one of the Midwest's largest book distributors, and he'd heard about the book. Could he come and see me?

Of course I was excited that such a respected businessman might be interested in my poem. But I also knew that Waldman's family heritage was Jewish. How would he possibly relate to my story?

When he showed up at my home, nervously I started to read aloud:

> *Like magic, I was six again*
> *deep in a Christmas spell,*
> *Steeped in a million memories*
> *the boy inside knew well.*

Ned Waldman shifted in his chair. As I read, he lowered his head and put his hand over his eyes. Was he dismayed at this waste of his valuable time? But then I saw his shoulders shake. He was crying.

When I finished reading, it was moments before he could speak. "I know all about Christmas," he said softly. "As a little boy, I celebrated it with a beloved woman who meant the world to me."

The story Ned Waldman told me could have made a book all its own.

When Ned was two months old, his mother died and his father left his family—for good. Ned's four-year-old brother went to live with an aunt. But baby Ned was left in the care of a kindly German Catholic woman who had been hired as the family's housekeeper shortly before Ned's mother's death. Her name was Adele Molitor.

Adele was divorced and had no children of her own. But she loved Ned with all her heart; and for the first five years of his life, Ned lived with her in a one-room apartment with a window overlooking an alley. Together they went everywhere, even to Mass.

At Christmastime, Ned sat with Adele as she addressed her Christmas cards. He told me he could still smell the special Christmas tea she brewed, fragrant with cinnamon and spices.

"Adele never forced her beliefs on me," Ned Waldman told me, "or tried to draw me away from my Jewish heritage. But the love she conveyed to me at Christmas I will never forget."

When Ned was five, he was taken away to live with his aunts, and he spent the rest of his childhood and teenage years with his Aunt Millie, another loving woman. But Adele Molitor continued to be a part of his life. She visited young Ned without fail every week until he was old enough to visit her.

Every December, the Waldman family would light Hanukkah candles. And in the days before Christmas, Ned would go to Adele's, where they would repeat the holiday traditions that meant so much to them.

As the years passed, Ned had children of his own. And every Christmas, after his own Hanukkah celebrations, he would take them to Adele's to trim the tree, sing "Silent Night" with Kate Smith, and have a cup of Christmas tea. Their get-togethers went on this way every Christmas until 1984, when Adele Molitor died.

"I don't remember details from my childhood about going to kindergarten or the playground," Ned said. "But I remember Christmas. And the love of the wonderful woman who introduced it to me. I want to publish your book as a tribute to her."

That was just the start of a friendship that has linked Warren Hanson, Ned Waldman, and me for the rest of our lives. Today we think of one another—and our wives and children—as family. And we rejoice about how a Presbyterian, a Lutheran, and a Jew were brought together because of the loving legacy of a Catholic.

The book has now sold over 500,000 copies. And people of all backgrounds and beliefs have called from all over the country to tell me how the poem has prompted them to visit older relatives and friends.

Want to do something monumental this holiday season? Call up someone you loved as a child—someone you haven't seen for a while, who might have trouble getting out and around. Go visit. Take that person by the hand. And settle in for a talk . . . over a cup of Christmas tea.

*Keep away from people who try to belittle
your ambitions. Small people always do that,
but the really great make you
feel that you, too, can become great.*

—Mark Twain

A Woman to Warm
Your Heart By

Dorothy Walworth

*I*n Cornwall, an old Hudson River town at the foot of Storm King Mountain, a story began fifty years ago and has not yet ended. When I visited there last winter, the older people of the town told me about it. It is a story they are proud to remember. "She is a woman to warm your heart by," they told me. "And as for him . . ."

That September, when it all started, Cornwall's seventy eighth-grade and high school pupils sat in a schoolroom only big enough for twenty, waiting for a new teacher from upstate—an old maid in her thirties named Frances Irene Hungerford.

One of the high school students was Steve Pigott, a tall and lanky seventeen-year-old. Steve was good at his studies, but his father didn't see what use school was. He kept telling Steve, "You're old enough to cut out that foolishness." Pat Pigott was an Irish immigrant farmer who couldn't read or write.

Everyone was nice to Steve, but there was a difference and he knew it. This was his second year in high school, and he figured it would be his last. When the other boys talked about how they were going to make something of themselves, Steve never said a word.

Miss Hungerford turned out to be so small that when Steve stretched out his arm, she could stand under it. But she stood straight as a footrule. She had steady deep-blue eyes, and when you looked into them you knew that all the winds over Storm King wouldn't budge her an inch. Her voice was pitched low, and her smile was like turning up a lamp.

One of the first things Miss Hungerford did was to write a sentence on the blackboard: "Seest thou the man who is diligent in his business? He shall stand before Kings." The schoolroom smothered giggles over that, as if anybody in Cornwall was ever going to get anywhere near a king!

In a week she had the high school wrapped around her little finger. If some of the boys had deviltry up their sleeves, she'd just smile; and her smile took the tuck right out of them. Every morning at assembly, the eighth grade and high school sang. Steve had a fine voice, and so did Miss Hungerford; and the songs got to be like duets between those two, with the other pupils piping away in the background.

After assembly, classes began. There weren't enough seats to go round so Miss Hungerford always gave somebody her chair and stood up all day. She taught every subject: French, German, algebra, history, English. She always gave her pupils the feeling that she learned with them. "Tell me about the Battle of Lake Erie," she'd say. "I'm curious to know."

"She's a *dedicated* sort of woman," people said, watching her walk back and forth from her boardinghouse to the school, always with a load of books on her arm. She went to church twice on Sundays and to prayer meeting Wednesday nights. But she never said a word about religion, except for that sentence on the blackboard. She just sort of lived it. Everyone has wondered since just what there was about Miss Hungerford that fired her pupils so. Somehow she made them believe they lived in a fine world, where a miracle could happen any morning, and they were fortunate and wonderful, with a lot of talent. "We've never thought so well of ourselves since," the Cornwall people say. And she sent out from that school a batch of youngsters who became important men and women all over the country.

Miss Hungerford took trouble with everybody, but she worked hardest with Steve. He stayed on in high school. She told him over and over that books were important; they were doors. Steve began wondering if there might be a door for him. Especially the spring of his senior year when they were reading "The Vision of Sir Launfal."

"A vision is a dream," Miss Hungerford told him one night after school while he was clapping chalk dust out of the blackboard erasers. "My dream is always to stay with boys and girls and books. What is yours, Stephen?"

He said to her then what he'd never said to a living soul: "I want to be a marine engineer."

He thought she'd laugh, but she sat there with her eyes sparkling. "You *can* be a marine engineer," she said. "All you need is the will to do it."

She had to give him faith in himself little by little. When she finally got Steve to speak to his father about going to college, Pat Pigott said Steve was crazy. Miss Hungerford was stubborn, though, and when fall came Steve went to Columbia University to take the mechanical engineering course.

He earned his way by working in a trolley barn; he sang in a church choir for five dollars a Sunday and did all sorts of odd jobs, studying whenever he could. Every time he got to thinking he ought to give the whole thing up, he'd slip away to Cornwall; and Miss Hungerford would somehow pour courage into him.

Stephen Pigott was the president of the class in his junior year; he edited the engineering-school publication; he sang in the university glee club; he was elected to a Greek-letter fraternity. And when he graduated in 1903, Miss Hungerford sent him a telegram: "I told you so." In 1908, Steve went to Scotland to help install a Curtis turbine for John Brown & Company, Ltd., the big shipbuilding firm that built the *Mauritania* and the *Lusitania*. He had planned to remain only four months, but the company persuaded him to stay on. In 1938, he became managing director of the company. He had designed the machinery for more than 300 British ships: cruisers, submarines, the *Hood*, the *Duke of York*, the *Queen Mary*.

During these thirty years Steve and Miss Hungerford kept up their friendship, writing to each other almost every week.

On the *Queen Mary's* maiden voyage Steve came back to America for a few days. Columbia was giving him an honorary degree; the American Society of Mechanical Engineers was awarding him a medal.

When he went to Cornwall the whole town turned out to meet him, and he made a speech in the big new high school. Everyone expected him to talk about his work or the fine people he had met abroad. But what he talked about was Miss Hungerford.

"Few men have been blessed with a friendship such as she has given to me for nearly half a century," he said. "When I have felt pride in any accomplished work, the things she said to me have been in my heart."

Miss Hungerford was now teaching in an upstate town near the shore of Lake Ontario. When Steve telephoned to say that he was coming to see her, he was told she was seriously ill and was advised not to make the visit. And so he had to sail without seeing her.

Steve is Sir Stephen Pigott now; he was knighted in 1939, about the time he designed the machinery for the *Queen Elizabeth.*

Miss Hungerford, now eighty-five, is still living in her upstate town, where she had kept on working until she was almost eighty. A few years ago, her town dedicated to her the Frances Irene Hungerford Library, "in appreciation of her fineness of character, her devotion to her work, and the lasting impression she has made."

That was the story they told me in Cornwall. It made me wonder what it was about Miss Hungerford that had made people remember her all their lives. So a few weeks ago, I went upstate to spend a day with her.

She came running down the front steps to meet me, light as a feather. Her hair is snow-white, but her eyes are the same deep blue. Even after what the Cornwall people had told me, I was not prepared for how tiny she is. Or how radiantly alive.

Her home is like her: tiny, cheerful, neat as a new pin. She showed me all over it, moving with quick, firm steps like a girl. In the book-filled sitting room I sat in her Boston rocker while she talked to me about Sir Stephen. She had newspaper clippings, pictures, Christmas cards, fifty years of his letters.

But though I tried all day, I couldn't get Miss Hungerford to talk about herself. She was willing to tell only about her old pupils, calling each one by name. We had high tea at her grandmother's fine old table, and she asked a blessing. We spoke of how Sir Stephen had promised to come to see her when the war is over, of how he had written in his last letter: "Wait for me, Miss Hungerford."

"I hope," she said, "that I can live long enough to see Stephen again."

"Why, Miss Hungerford," I said, "you'll live forever!"

"I know that," she answered gravely, "but I may soon be out of touch with all you people for a little while."

When the car came for me, we walked to the curb together, her hand laid lightly on my arm. And then, for the first time, she spoke about herself. "You know, I feel ashamed," she said, "when I see all these bright modern teachers. Compared to them, I was not very well trained." She paused; her hand tightened on my arm. "You see, all I had was love."

Years and years of happiness
only make us realize how lucky we are
to have friends that have shared
and made that happiness a reality.
—ROBERT E. FREDERICK

LONG-DISTANCE FRIENDS

PAMELA KENNEDY

I was browsing in a gift shop the other day and a small wall hanging caught my eye. On a piece of rough board the artist had painted a colorful garden. Small lavender violets clustered in front of a row of daisies. Behind these, roses and snapdragons bloomed. A line of sunflowers stood guard at the garden's border, and in the distance a sheltering barrier of evergreens filled the background. Arched over the top of the plaque were the words "Friendship Is Life's Garden."

This idea of friendship as a garden intrigued me. I mentally inventoried my friends, deciding who was a sensitive violet, who a cheerful daisy, which ones were elegant roses, and which were practical and optimistic sunflowers. I must admit I even ventured to identify a few weeds in my musings! Then I recalled the row of trees standing in the background of the artist's scene. I'm not sure if these were meant to be included in friendship's garden, but for me they became a powerful image of a very special kind of friend I treasure—my long-distance friends.

Thirty years of marriage to a military man have offered many wonderful opportunities to make new friends and an equal number of occasions to leave them behind as we moved thousands of miles away to a new assignment. Some of my more stationary acquaintances doubt the possibility of maintaining friendships with people one doesn't see for years. I like to tell them distance isn't really a barrier to friendship; it only adds a new dimension to it.

Like the trees in the artist's picture, my long-distance friends offer a sense of perspective to my life. I can see them in memories that tower above the circumstances of today, reminding me of times we shared joy, challenge, sadness, and triumph together. Just like the wind and rain and sun shape the development of a tree, my friends helped to shape me by their influence, example, and encouragement.

I met Nan when she was a patient in a hospital where I was doing volunteer work about twenty-five years ago. I felt so sorry for this beautiful mother of six because she suffered from constant pain and was confined to a wheelchair. With the thought of cheering her up, I visited her often, and we spent several hours sharing our thoughts on life and faith. I'm not sure if my immature attempts to offer solace accomplished much in her life, but her wit and wisdom made a profound difference in mine. She gently demonstrated that true joy and peace are more a matter of internal circumstances than external, that a deep and abiding confidence in God transcends our present doubts, and that family is the context in which we learn about love—both giving and receiving. Her words strengthened me like the nourishing rain strengthens the trunk of a tree, enabling it to grow until it is able to withstand a storm without being broken. I have seen Nan only a handful of times since we were first friends; but each time I feel tested by the winds of a storm, I recall her strength and am encouraged to endure with her grace.

Another friend, Terry, was with me twenty years ago when my second son was born. My husband was overseas, and Terry filled in as my labor and delivery coach. She and I shared an incredible experience and will always be joined by that bond of birth. When her army husband was transferred overseas, I grieved like I was losing a member of my family. Although we corresponded by mail, it was fifteen years before we met again; and when that happened we picked up as if we had only been apart for a few weeks! Our children had grown, our lives and circumstances had changed; but, like the towering evergreens, our roots are intertwined at a deep level, and we will always be together there.

In a small Wisconsin town several years ago, Lynn and I raised toddlers together. We shared all the triumphs and trials of toilet training, tumbles, and temper tantrums. We debated the merits of breast and bottle, whole grain and processed, scheduling and spontaneity. At one time we saw each other several times a day, but now we are fortunate to visit once every few years. Our children are now young men and women, but our mutual experiences as new mothers still bind the two of us together. Like the trees we stand apart, but when the winds of chance and circumstance allow, our branches touch once more and our lives intermingle again like the fragrant boughs.

In the garden of friendship, the colorful blossoms blooming the closest may get the lion's share of our attention, but I have learned to also treasure the trees standing in the background. Just like that row of evergreens in the artist's painting, long-distance friends provide both perspective and beauty: the perspective of the past and the beauty of shared memories adding a depth of experience to our lives that only time and patience can produce.

And he shall be unto thee a restorer of thy life,
and a nourisher of thine old age.
—RUTH 4:15

MEMORIES KEEP
OUR SPIRITS YOUNG

MARJORIE HOLMES

I remember the Sunday in church when I first realized my father was getting old. He and Mother were visiting us, and we'd taken them to our Episcopal church, where they didn't feel at home. There was a crowd and we had to sit up front, and Dad wasn't prepared when the collection plate was passed. His uncertain hands trembled as he reached in embarrassment for his pocketbook—an old-fashioned snap pouch—and struggled to get it open and find some coins for the offering.

I took Dad's hands in mine. His hands had always been so strong, hands of authority and conviction. Wagging, playful hands, kind hands fixing things, hands you could depend on. I could feel Dad's discomfort and wondered what to do.

But when the service was over, the minister came down the steps to Dad and embraced him. It turned out that he and Dad had been boyhood friends and had often chased each other through the countryside. They shared their memories, and soon both of them were laughing.

The inroads of age are inevitable, but our friends—and our memories—can help us keep our spirits young.

Famous Friendships

A companion loves some agreeable qualities which a man may possess, but a friend loves the man himself.
—JAMES BOSWELL

HE HAD AN IMMENSE STOCK OF COMMON SENSE

JOSEPH GILLESPIE

*H*e was genial but not very sociable. He did not seek company but when he was in it he was the most entertaining person I ever knew. . . .

His love of wealth was very weak. I asked him how much land he owned. He said that the house and lot he lived on and one forty-acre tract were all the real estate he owned and that he got the forty for his services in the Black Hawk War. I inquired why he never speculated in land and pointed to a tract that I had located with a land-warrant that cost me ninety cents an acre. He said he had no capacity whatever for speculation and never attempted it. All the use Mr. Lincoln had for wealth was to enable him to appear respectable. He never hoarded nor wasted but used money as he needed it and gave himself little or no concern about laying up.

He was the most indulgent parent I ever knew. His children literally ran over him, and he was powerless to withstand their importunities. He was remarkably tender of the feelings of others and never wantonly offended even the most despicable although he was a man of great nerve when aroused. I have seen him on several occasions display great heroism when the circumstances seemed to demand it. He was very sensitive where he thought he had failed to come up to the expectations of his friends. I remember a case. He was pitted by the Whigs in 1840 to debate with Mr. Douglas, the Democratic champion. Lincoln did not come up to the requirements of the occasion. He was conscious of his failure and I never saw any man so much distressed. He begged to be permitted to try it again and was reluctantly indulged, and in the next effort, he transcended our highest expectations. I never heard and never expect to hear such a triumphant vindication as he then gave of Whig measures or policy. He never after, to my knowledge, fell below himself.

Mr. Lincoln had the appearance of being a slow thinker. My impression is that he was not so slow as he was careful. He never liked to put forth a proposition without revolving it over in his own mind; but when he was compelled to act promptly, as in debate, he was quick enough. Douglas, who was a very skillful controversialist, never obtained any advantage over him. I never could discover anything in Mr. Lincoln's mental composition remarkably singular. His qualities were those ordinarily given to mankind but he had them in remarkable degree. He was wonderfully kind, careful, and just. He had an immense stock of common sense, and he had faith enough to trust it in every emergency. He had passed through all the grades of society when he reached the Presidency, and he had found common sense a sure reliance and he put it into practice. He acted all through his career upon just such principles as every man of good common sense would approve and say, "that is just as I would have done myself." There was nothing of the Napoleonic in his style of doing things. If he had been in Napoleon's place, he never would have gone off to Egypt to strike a blow at England, and he would have been equally careful not to send an army to Moscow. Lincoln had no superhuman qualities (which we call genius), but he had those which belong to mankind generally in an astonishing degree.

There was a tinge of sadness in Mr. Lincoln's composition. He was not naturally disposed to look on the bright side of the picture. He felt very strongly that there was more of discomfort than real happiness in human existence under the most favorable circumstances, and the general current of his reflections was in that channel. He never obtruded these views upon others, but on the contrary strove as much as possible to be gay and lively. There was a slight dash of what is generally called superstition in Mr. Lincoln's mind. He evidently believed that the perceptions were sometimes more unerring than reason and outstripped it. I can't say that he believed in presentiments, but he undoubtedly had gloomy forebodings as to himself. He told me after his election that he did not count confidentially, on living to get through with the task set before him. And I did not think that he apprehended death in the natural way; still I do not believe that he took any precautions to guard against danger. I met him once, coming alone from the war office to the White House, and remarked to him that I thought he was exposing himself to danger of assassination. He replied that no precautions he could take would be availing if they were determined to kill him. I rode out with him that evening to the Soldiers' Home [Lincoln's summer residence], when he was accompanied by an escort of cavalry. On the way he said that the escort was rather forced upon him by the military men, that he could see no certain protection against assassination if it was determined to take away his life. He said it seemed to him like putting up the gap in only one place when the fence was down all along.

If instead of a gem, or even a flower,
we should cast the gift of a loving thought
into the heart of a friend,
that would be giving as the angels give.
—George Macdonald

Literary Friends

William Dean Howells

*W*hen Longfellow read verse, it was with a hollow, with a mellow resonant murmur, like the note of some deep-throated horn. His voice was very lulling in quality, and at the Dante Club it used to have early effect with an old scholar who sat in a cavernous armchair at the corner of the fire and who drowsed audibly in the soft tone and the gentle heat. The poet had a fat terrier who wished always to be present at the meetings of the Club, and he commonly fell asleep at the same moment with that dear old scholar, so that when they began to make themselves heard in concert, one could not tell which it was that most took our thoughts from the text of *Paradiso*. When the duet opened, Longfellow would look up with an arch recognition of the fact and then go gravely on to the end of the canto. At the close he would speak to his friend and lead him out to supper as if he had not seen or heard anything amiss.

The supper was very plain: a cold turkey, which the host carved, or a haunch of venison, or some braces of grouse, or a platter of quails, with a deep bowl of salad, and the sympathetic companionship of those elect vintages which Longfellow loved, and which he chose with the inspiration of affection. We usually began with oysters, and when some one who was expected did not come promptly, Longfellow invited us to raid his plate as a just punishment of his delay. One evening, Lowell remarked, with the cayenne poised above his blue-points, "It's astonishing how fond these fellows are of pepper."

The old friend of the cavernous armchair was perhaps not wide enough awake to repress an "ah?" of deep interest in this fact of natural history, and Lowell was provoked to go on. "Yes, I've dropped a red pepper pod into a barrel of them, before now, and then taken them out in a solid mass, clinging to it like a swarm of bees to their queen."

"Is it possible?" cried the old friend; and then Longfellow intervened to save him from worse, and turned the talk.

—

No doubt he had his resentments, but he hushed them in his heart, which he did not suffer them to embitter. While Poe was writing of "Longfellow and Other Plagiarists," Longfellow was helping to keep Poe alive by the loans which always made themselves gifts in Poe's case . . .

He was patient of all things, and gentle beyond all mere gentlemanliness. But it would have been a great mistake to mistake his mildness for softness . . . If he did not find it well to assert himself, he was prompt in behalf of his friends, and one of the fine things told of him was his resenting some censures of Sumner at a dinner in Boston during the old pro-slavery times: he said to the gentlemen present that Sumner was his friend, and he must leave their company if they continued to assail him.

—

At the services held in the house before the obsequies at the cemetery, I saw the poet for the last time, where "Dead he lay among his books," in the library behind his study . . . All who were left of his old Cambridge were present, and among those who had come farther was Emerson. He went up to the bier, and with his arms crossed on his breast, and his elbows held in either hand, stood with his head pathetically fallen forward, looking down at the dead face. Those who knew how his memory was a mere blank, with faint gleams of recognition capriciously coming and going in it, must have felt that he was struggling to remember who it was lay there before him; and for me the electly simple words confessing his failure will always be pathetic with his remembered aspect: "The gentleman we have just been burying," he said to the friend who had come with him, "was a sweet and beautiful soul; but I forget his name."

*God made the perfect and complete instrument: the human
voice. It gives you personality, individuality, words,
and music all in one vehicle.*

—HARRY VERPLOEGH

HOW I FOUND MY VOICE

JAMES EARL JONES

Today I am known for my voice as much as for my
acting. It has been my good fortune to receive jobs such as
the speaking role of Darth Vader in George Lucas's *Star Wars*
trilogy and the voice-over announcer for CNN cable television.
I also narrated Aaron Copland's Lincoln portrait on a compact
disc I recorded with the Seattle Symphony. Perhaps my greatest honor came when I was asked to read the New Testament
on tape.

But it took a long time to believe such good things could
happen to me. When I was a youngster I stuttered so badly I
was completely unable to speak in public.

Since I was eight I'd had trouble speaking. It was so bad that
whenever I stood up in class to read, the other kids snickered and
laughed. I always sat down, my face burning with shame.

I'm not sure what caused my stuttering. Perhaps it was an
emotional problem. I was born in Arkabutla, Mississippi, and
when I was about five, I moved to live with my grandparents on
their farm near Dublin in northern Michigan. It was traumatic
moving from the warm, easy ways of catfish country to the
harsh climate of the north, where people seemed so different.

Fortunately, my granddaddy was a gentle man, a farmer
who taught me to love the land. He was short and he had a
prodigious amount of energy. He even built a church to please

grandmother, a fervent worshiper of the Lord. All sorts of people were invited to our little church; white, black and American Indian came together in a nondenominational fellowship. Granddad's Irish heritage came out in his love for language; during the week he used "everyday talk," but on Sunday he spoke only the finest English.

As much as I admired his fluency, I couldn't come close to it. I finally quit Sunday school and church, not wanting to be humiliated anymore. All through my grade school years, the only way the teacher could assess my progress was for me to write down everything I had learned.

Oh, I could talk, all right. Our farm animals knew that. I found it easy to call the pigs, tell the dogs to round up the cows, and vent my feelings to Fanny, the horse whose big brown eyes and lifted ears seemed to express interest in all I said. But when visitors came and I was asked to say hello, I could only stand, pound my feet, and grit my teeth. That awful feeling of my voice being trapped got worse as I grew older.

Then, when I was fourteen, Professor Donald Crouch came to our school. He was a retired college professor who had settled in nearby Brethren, a Mennonite community. When he heard that our agricultural high was teaching Chaucer, Shakespeare, and other classics, he couldn't stand not being a part of our school. So he left his retreat to teach us English, history, and Latin.

Donald Crouch was a tall, lean man with gray hair; English was his favorite subject, poetry his deepest love. He'd been an associate of Robert Frost. He held a book of poems as if it were a diamond necklace, turning pages as if uncovering treasures. He memorized a poem every day, explaining that if he ever lost his eyesight he would still be able to savor all that beauty.

When he learned that I not only loved poetry but was writing it, we found a kinship. There was, however, one difficulty between us. Professor Crouch (we always called him that) could not stand the fact I refused to read my poems to the class.

"Jim, poetry is meant to be read aloud, just like sermons," he pressed. "You should be able to speak those beautiful words."

I shook my head and turned away.

Then he tricked me. I labored long and hard on a poem, and after handing it in I waited expectantly for his critique. It didn't come. Instead, one day as the students assembled, he challenged me. "Jim, I don't think you wrote this."

I stared at him in disbelief. "Why," I started, anger flooding me, "course I did!"

"Well, then," he said, "you've got to prove it by getting up and reciting it from memory."

By then the other students had settled at their desks. He looked at me meaningfully and nodded. With knees shaking, I walked up before my peers.

"Jim will recite his latest poem," announced Professor Crouch.

For a moment I stood breathless. I could see smirks and wry smiles on some faces. Then I began. And kept going. I recited my poem all the way through—without hesitation or fault! I stood amazed and floated back to my desk in a daze, amid wild applause.

Afterward, Professor Crouch congratulated me. "Aha," he said. "Now we have something here. Not only will you have to write more poetry and read it aloud to know how good it feels, but I'm sure that you will want to read other writers' poetry before the class."

I was dubious about that, but said I'd try.

Soon I began to discover something other stutterers know. Most have no problem singing because the lyrics' rhythmic pattern flows by itself. I found the same cadences in poetry, and before long my fellow students actually looked forward to hearing me recite. I loved the rolling beat of "The Song of Hiawatha," especially since I had Indian blood in my veins. "By the shores of Gitche Gummee," I recited. "By the shining Big-Sea-Waters . . ."

I discovered I did have a voice, a strong one. Under Professor Crouch's tutelage, I entered oratorical contests and debates. He never pushed anything at me again; he just wanted all his students to wake up. He never even pressed us with religion but figured if we did wake up we would find God, find our calling and, in so doing, find life.

As my stuttering disappeared, I began dreaming of becoming an actor, like my father, who was then performing in New York City. No one in my family had ever gone to college. But encouraged by Professor Crouch, I took exams and won a scholarship to the University of Michigan.

There I entered the drama department and after graduation fulfilled my ROTC responsibility by serving with the Army's Cold Weather Training Command on mountain maneuvers in Colorado. It was in the army that a Jesuit chaplain helped me understand who God really was and opened the door to which Professor Crouch had led me.

Later, on the GI Bill, I signed up with the American Theatre Wing in New York and supported myself between roles by sweeping floors of off-Broadway stages. In 1962 I earned an Obie for my role in an off-Broadway production of *Othello* and have been an actor ever since.

Meanwhile, I always kept in touch with my old professor,

by letter and telephone. Every time we talked it was always, "Hi, Jim. Read any good poetry lately?" He was losing his sight and I remembered his early explanation of why he had memorized poetry. In later years when I was doing Shakespeare's *Timon of Athens* at the Yale Repertory Theatre in New Haven, Connecticut, I phoned him.

"Can I fly you in from Michigan to see it?"

"Jim," he sighed, "I'm blind now. I'd hate not to be able to see you acting. It would hurt too much."

"I understand, Professor," I said, helped in part by the realization that though my mentor could no longer see, he was still living in a world vibrant with all of the beautiful treasures he had stored.

About two years later I learned Donald Crouch had passed on. I thanked God for all the professor's help and friendship.

And so, when I was asked to record the New Testament, I really did it for a tall, lean man with gray hair who had not only helped to guide me to the author of the Scriptures, but as the father of my resurrected voice, had also helped me find abundant life.

*My friends have made the story of my life. In a thousand
ways they have turned my limitations into beautiful
privileges and enabled me to walk serene and happy
in the shadow cast by my deprivation.*

—HELEN KELLER

FROM THE STORY OF MY LIFE

HELEN KELLER

The most important day I remember in all my life is the one on which my teacher, Anne Mansfield Sullivan, came to me. I am filled with wonder when I consider the immeasurable contrasts between the two lives which it connects. It was the third of March, 1887, three months before I was seven years old.

On the afternoon of that eventful day, I stood on the porch, dumb, expectant. I guessed vaguely from my mother's signs and from the hurrying to and fro in the house that something unusual was about to happen, so I went to the door and waited on the steps. The afternoon sun penetrated the mass of honeysuckle that covered the porch and fell on my upturned face. My fingers lingered almost unconsciously on the familiar leaves and blossoms which had just come forth to greet the sweet Southern spring. I did not know what the future held of marvel or surprise for me. Anger and bitterness had preyed upon me continually for weeks, and a deep languor had succeeded this passionate struggle.

Have you ever been at sea in a dense fog, when it seemed as if a tangible white darkness shut you in, and the great ship, tense and anxious, groped her way toward the shore with plummet and sounding line, and you waited with beating heart for something to happen? I was like that ship before my education began, only

I was without compass or sounding line and had no way of knowing how near the harbor was. "Light! Give me light!" was the wordless cry of my soul, and the light of love shone on me in that very hour.

I felt approaching footsteps. I stretched out my hand as I supposed to my mother. Someone took it, and I was caught up and held close in the arms of her who had come to reveal all things to me and, more than all things else, to love me.

The morning after my teacher came, she led me into her room and gave me a doll. The little blind children at the Perkins Institution had sent it and Laura Bridgman had dressed it; but I did not know this until afterward. When I had played with it a little while, Miss Sullivan slowly spelled into my hand the word "d-o-l-l." I was at once interested in this finger play and tried to imitate it. When I finally succeeded in making the letters correctly I was flushed with childish pleasure and pride. Running downstairs to my mother I held up my hand and made the letters for doll. I did not know that I was spelling a word or even that words existed; I was simply making my fingers go in monkey-like imitation. In the days that followed I learned to spell in this uncomprehending way a great many words, among them pin, hat, cup, and a few verbs like sit, stand, and walk. But my teacher had been with me several weeks before I understood that everything has a name.

One day, while I was playing with my new doll, Miss Sullivan put my big rag doll into my lap also, spelled "d-o-l-l" and tried to make me understand that "d-o-l-l" applied to both. Earlier in the day we had had a tussle over the words "m-u-g" and "w-a-t-e-r." Miss Sullivan had tried to impress it upon me that "m-u-g" is mug and that "w-a-t-e-r" is water, but I persisted in confounding the two. In despair she had dropped the subject for the time, only to renew it at the first opportunity. I became impatient at her repeated attempts and, seizing the new doll, I dashed it upon the floor. I was keenly delighted when I felt the fragments of the broken doll at my feet. Neither sorrow nor regret followed my passionate outburst. I had not loved the doll. In the still, dark world in which I lived, there was no strong sentiment or tenderness. I felt my teacher sweep the fragments to one side of the hearth, and I had a sense of satisfaction that the cause of my discomfort was removed. She brought me my hat, and I knew I was going out into the warm sunshine. This thought, if a wordless sensation may be called a thought, made me hop and skip with pleasure.

We walked down the path to the well house, attracted by the fragrance of the honeysuckle with which it was covered. Someone was drawing water and my teacher placed my hand under the spout. As the cool stream gushed over one hand she spelled into the other the word water, first slowly, then rapidly. I stood still, my whole attention fixed upon the motions of her fingers. Suddenly I felt a misty consciousness as of something forgotten—a thrill of returning thought; and somehow the mystery of language was revealed to me. I knew then that "w-a-t-e-r" meant the wonderful cool something that was flowing over my hand. That living word awakened my soul, gave it light, hope, joy, set it free! There were barriers still, it is true, but barriers that could in time be swept away.

I left the well house eager to learn. Everything had a name, and each name gave birth to a new thought. As we returned to the house, every object which I touched seemed to quiver with life. That was because I saw everything with the strange, new sight that had come to me. On entering the door I remembered the doll I had broken. I felt my way to the hearth and picked up the pieces. I tried vainly to put them together. Then my eyes filled with tears; for I realized what I had done, and for the first time I felt repentance and sorrow.

I learned a great many new words that day. I do not remember what they all were; but I do know that mother, father, sister, teacher were among them—words that were to make the world blossom for me, "like Aaron's rod, with flowers." It would have been difficult to find a happier child than I was as I lay in my crib at the close of that eventful day and lived over the joys it had brought me, and for the first time longed for a new day to come.

Others there are whose hands have sunbeams in them,
so that their grasp warms my heart.

—HELEN KELLER

ON HELEN

ANNE MANSFIELD SULLIVAN

Anne Mansfield Sullivan writes in her letters
of the changes taking place in Helen Keller.

March 20, 1887

*M*y heart is singing for joy this morning. A miracle has happened! The light of understanding has shone upon my little pupil's mind, and behold, all things are changed!

The wild little creature of two weeks ago has been transformed into a gentle child. She is sitting by me as I write, her face serene and happy, crocheting a long red chain of Scotch wool. She learned the stitch this week and is very proud of the achievement. When she succeeded in making a chain that would reach across the room, she patted herself on the arm and put the first work of her hands lovingly against her cheek. She lets me kiss her now, and when she is in a particularly gentle mood, she will sit in my lap for a minute or two; but she does not return my caresses. The great step—the step that counts—has been taken. The little savage has learned her first lesson in obedience and finds the yoke easy. It now remains my pleasant task to direct and mold the beautiful intelligence that is beginning to stir in the child-soul. Already people remark the change in Helen. Her father looks in at us morning and evening as he goes to and from his office, and sees her contentedly stringing her beads or making horizontal lines on her sewing card, and exclaims, "How quiet she is!" When I came, her movements were so insistent that one always felt there was something unnatural and almost weird about her. I have noticed also that she eats much less, a fact which troubles her father so much that he is anxious to get her home. He says she is homesick. I don't agree with him; but I suppose we shall have to leave our little bower very soon.

Helen has learned several nouns this week. "M-u-g" and "m-i-l-k," have given her more trouble than other words. When she spells milk, she points to the mug, and when she spells mug, she makes the sign for pouring or drinking, which shows that she has confused the words. She has no idea yet that everything has a name.

—

April 5, 1887

I must write you a line this morning because something very important has happened. Helen has taken the second great step in her education. She has learned that everything has a name and that the manual alphabet is the key to everything she wants to know.

—

In a previous letter I think I wrote you that "mug" and milk" had given Helen more trouble than all the rest. She confused the nouns with the verb "drink." She didn't know the word for "drink" but went through the pantomime of drinking whenever she spelled "mug" or "milk." This morning, while she was washing, she wanted to know the name for "water." When she wants to know the name of anything, she points to it and pats my hand. I spelled "w-a-t-e-r" and thought no more about it until after breakfast. Then it occurred to me that with the help of this new word I might succeed in straightening out the "mug-milk" difficulty. We went out to the pump house, and I made Helen hold her mug under the spout while I pumped. As the cold water gushed forth, filling the mug, I spelled "w-a-t-e-r" in Helen's free hand. The word coming so close upon the sensation of cold water rushing over her hand seemed to startle her. She dropped the mug and stood as one transfixed. A new light came into her face. She spelled "water" several times. Then she dropped on the ground and asked for its name and pointed to the pump and the trellis, and suddenly turning round she asked for my name. I spelled "Teacher." Just then the nurse brought Helen's little sister into the pump house, and Helen spelled "baby" and pointed to the nurse. All the way back to the house she was highly excited and learned the name of every object she touched, so that in a few hours she had added thirty new words to her vocabulary. Here are some of them: Door, open, shut, give, go, come, and a great many more.

P.S. I didn't finish my letter in time to get it posted last night; so I shall add a line. Helen got up this morning like a radiant fairy. She has flitted from object to object, asking the name of everything and kissing me for very gladness. Last night when I got in bed, she stole into my arms of her own accord and kissed me for the first time, and I thought my heart would burst, so full was it of joy.

A real friend is one who helps us to think our noblest
thoughts, put forth our best efforts, and to be our best selves.
—AUTHOR UNKNOWN

A USEFUL FRIENDSHIP

NANCY SKARMEAS

*E*leanor Roosevelt was not entirely comfortable on board her husband's 1920 vice-presidential campaign train. The days were long and the living quarters cramped and spartan. Although she had longed for years to be involved in her husband's political life, on the train Eleanor felt out of place and isolated from the purposes of the campaign. By day, Franklin gave speeches, shook hands with voters, and conferred with advisers; in the evenings he planned strategy and played poker with the other men at the back of the train. Eleanor felt of little use.

Also aboard that train was Louis Howe, Franklin Roosevelt's campaign manager and friend. For years, Louis had been a frequent guest at the Roosevelt home; and while Franklin had always welcomed his friend, Eleanor had merely tolerated him. Howe had a brilliant political mind and was devoted to the advancement of Franklin's career; but he was a small, unsightly man, and his disheveled appearance and rough manner disturbed Eleanor's sense of reserve and propriety.

Connected only through Franklin, the two existed in different worlds. Eleanor lived a private, domestic life with her five children. Howe immersed himself in politics, particularly the politics of Franklin Delano Roosevelt. Their worlds intersected but never truly touched each other. Not until the 1920 campaign, when circumstances gave Louis Howe a chance to see the quiet, dedicated intelligence of Eleanor Roosevelt, did Eleanor learn that beneath the rough exterior of Louis Howe was a true friend.

Eleanor Roosevelt—thirty-five years old and unaccustomed to life away from her home and family—was ready for a friend in her life. With five children to care for, a husband consumed by his own political ambitions, and a domineering mother-in-law reluctant to relinquish control of any aspect of family life to her son's wife, Eleanor had little encouragement to indulge her own growing interest in politics and public life. But the interest was sincere and strong, and she had boarded the campaign train full of hope for a new chapter in her life, if perhaps a bit troubled by self-doubt in the face of the unfamiliar.

Louis Howe was, on the exterior, exactly the man that Eleanor Roosevelt saw—a chain-smoking, untidy, unrefined man. But he was also a man of great sensitivity and insight. Howe sensed Eleanor's discomfort and loneliness; he saw that she lacked confidence in her public self. What he also saw were her intelligence and her good judgment. On the campaign trail that year he appealed to these traits. He brought Eleanor drafts of her husband's speeches and asked for her opinions. He looked to her for guidance on the "women's viewpoint," so important in 1920, the first year of the vote for women. He not only included her in the business of her husband's campaign, he gave her a voice of her own.

When the campaign ended, Franklin had lost the election, but Eleanor had gained an ally; no more was Howe simply rough or unsightly, he was a friend. In the next years, Eleanor emerged as a public figure in her own right; and every step of the way, Louis Howe was there. He encouraged her interest in politics—not as the wife of a politician but as an influential, individual voice. He coached her in public speaking, served as her literary agent, and taught her the skills of newspaper publishing.

Such encouragement, apparently, was all that Eleanor needed. When her husband was stricken with polio in 1921, she picked up the slack, keeping the Roosevelt name alive in New York politics. She became a leader in the League of Women Voters, the Women's Trade Union, the Leslie Commission, and the New York Democratic State Committee. She gave radio addresses, wrote articles and editorials, and was active in the fight for women's rights. She became, in other words, the Eleanor Roosevelt who is admired and emulated today, a woman of strength and grace with an unfailing commitment to public service.

Louis Howe was a part of Eleanor's life for the remainder of his own life. When Franklin was elected President, Eleanor experienced a return of the old self-doubts; she worried that her usefulness would be destroyed by her role as first lady. Howe, as always, had no doubts. In fact, without the least bit of condescension, he assured Eleanor that not only could she be first lady, she could be president. He believed in her and never allowed her to lose her belief in herself.

Eleanor Roosevelt once told an interviewer that the most honored goal one could pursue was the "privilege of being useful." Louis Howe gave her the confidence she needed to become useful and, through his commitment to his friend, proved his own usefulness. We can ask no better standard in choosing our own friends than that set by Eleanor Roosevelt and Louis Howe. Their friendship is proof that our greatest friends do more than simply mirror back to us the person that they see, rather they see beyond the present to the person we can become.

Blessed are they who have the gift of making friends,
for it is one of God's best gifts. It involves many things,
but above all, the power of going out of one's self
and appreciating whatever is noble and loving in another.
—Thomas Hughes

A Noble Relation

Richard Wagner

Franz Liszt, nineteenth-century Hungarian piano virtuoso and
composer, enjoyed a long-lived friendship with fellow music lover
Richard Wagner, a German composer of the same era.

My Dearest Liszt,
I must say, you are a friend. Let me say no more to you, for although I always recognized in friendship between men the noblest and highest relation, it was you who embodied this idea into its fullest reality by letting me no longer imagine, but feel and grasp, what a friend is.

I do not thank you, for you alone have the power to thank yourself by your joy in being what you are. It is noble to have a friend, but still nobler to be a friend.

Our Friends
Next Door

It does us good to enjoy the comfort of friends.
—AUTHOR UNKNOWN

A COUNTRYWOMAN'S JOURNAL

GLADYS TABER

January

*T*here is, I have found, at least one good or lovely thing in every single day. Everyone has sorrow, endures difficult times, but loveliness abides if we look for it. I almost forgot this the time I wrenched my knee and was flat for two weeks. I picked the worst time, too, for Erma Vanek, my mainstay, was down with a virus. Joe, her husband, had to take on all of their chores besides his regular job. The weather was terrible. It does seem as if things pile up sometimes. I helped matters by getting bursitis in both shoulders from trying to make my way to the kitchen (despite that wrenched knee), clinging to furniture tops for support. After that bout, I found I could not even turn over in bed.

Of course, this wasn't a major disaster, but when you live alone, walking assumes extra importance, and I felt very low after my unsuccessful attempt. And then, just at the worst moment, in walked my neighbor, Wilma Phillips, bringing my mail. She let the dogs out, let them in, fixed me a tray, and lugged my books over near my bed so that I could reach them. And at six that night my bedroom door opened: there was Steve Nies—from up the hill—with a hot dinner wrapped in foil. His mother had dished mine up with theirs, and the sugar-sweet ham, fluffy potatoes, and fresh peas were flanked by an artistic salad. Dessert was in a foil cup. I have seldom had a happier time. Long after I forgot the misery of the pain, I felt the warm glow of friendship. By the time I could hobble, I felt like a queen.

George, at the market, offered to bring me, personally, any groceries I needed. Dick Gracy, from the Main Road, brought my newspaper right into the kitchen and hauled supplies. Joe carried wood, opened stuck windows, and went to the woods to pick me the loveliest bouquet of spring flowers I have ever seen. So, when I finally landed in the hospital, I had plenty of courage for that.

This being my first time out of circulation, except for brief bouts with grippe, I learned something important. It isn't the occasional grand gesture that matters so much. My neighbors were never too busy *every day* to pop in and look after me. The first minute Erma could get out of bed and weave over, bringing my favorite chicken soup as only she makes it, I was able to assure her I was fine, even if I could only take four steps.

I have several very dear friends who tell me they expect nothing but trouble. I do not go along with this. I do not believe in living trouble before it happens. I prefer to remember the loving-kindness of friends and expect this never to fail. I believe life is rich and rewarding, provided we accept it.

—

August

Most of my special hours have to do with friendship, I find. When Faith Baldwin comes, we often drive around following back roads with Holly sniffing gustily out the back window. I wish I knew the wonderful world of smell as she does. If we stop to eat, we choose a place where we can watch Holly, and this does limit the choice. I suppose there aren't too many people who would lure an Irish setter from her own car and steal her, but how do I know?

Recently on a late Sunday afternoon Steve and Olive asked me to join them for a drive. We headed toward the Berkshires, with no particular destination; we just took any road that looked inviting. We passed dreaming villages, tranquil farms, deep woods. We found a stand of white birches such as we did not know existed. We came to violet hills, folding into the deeper sky. When we stopped by a trout stream, Olive produced red caviar and onion sandwiches, thin-sliced ham and Swiss cheese, and frosty glasses of iced drinks. We drove home through a shadowy world, in which, as Olive said, nobody was about at all. We said little, just absorbing that wonderful quiet. Memory of those hours of companionship will warm me next winter when the wind roars and the snow piles up. I try to collect happy times and can highly recommend such a collection. It is far better than collecting troubled hours.

My young friend Tommy has also given me many happy memories. One of the most precious moments was the time he arrived at my door with a birthday cake, which he had baked for me himself. It was a beautiful cake! While it lasted, he came over every afternoon and we lit the candles and ate two more pieces.

Some memories of friendship we especially cherish because that friend is no longer with us. Dr. Ghiselin was more than a doctor to Jill and me; he was our very good and dear friend from the day his shingle went up in our village. When this beloved physician died suddenly, everyone felt great sorrow, for this was a truly great man who actually gave his life in the service of the community. I think the loss of a good physician is hard to accept for many reasons. One feels humanity itself is the loser, for the endless years of work that go into the making of a doctor cannot be bequeathed to some new medical student. This is a road every man travels alone if he needs must take it.

———

November

One morning I wake up and all my little summertime friends have flown away. At the feeder, chickadees, nuthatches, blue jays, and woodpeckers are bustling about, reminding me of returned vacationers settling in after a long time away. With the snow come the juncoes—often called snowbirds—small, trim cloud-gray birds, with pearl-pink bills and faintly pink breasts. They arrive in flocks and are ground feeders. One thing puzzles me. Whenever I picked up Robert, the quail who lived with Dr. and Mrs. Kienzle on the Cape, I noticed that her tiny feet were cold as icicles; but they warmed up quickly if she remained in my hand. Therefore, I figure, the circulation of other birds should be the same. So why don't the juncoes' feet freeze as these little birds hop around in the snow?

I also wonder why delicate songbirds don't migrate in winter or hibernate. Their normal temperature, I'm told, is 101 degrees (and we think we're ill when we have that much of a temperature). The chickadees will fly to the feeder in a driving snowstorm and chatter cheerfully as they crack sunflower seeds, while I hunt up my snow boots and mittens before venturing outside.

The relationship between birds and man can be a rewarding one, for even the shyest of them respond to gestures of friendship. The distance between my little visitors and me has been bridged by the offering of sunflower seeds, chickfeed, raisins, suet cakes, and bread crumbs. As I talk softly, I am answered by the fluttering of wings and a dipping toward my hands. I cannot help thinking that barriers between people could also be bridge by the extending of an open hand.

With merry company, the dreary way is endured.
—Spanish Proverb

Adventures on the No. 5 Bus

Mary Ann O'Roark

I was six years old when I took my first bus ride. It was on a visit to my grandmother in Steubenville, Ohio. We hurried up the hollyhock-lined alley to the stop and climbed aboard the rumbling city bus. Grandma Paisley greeted the driver by name. I watched out the window as we rode down past the Bond Bread sign (you could smell the bread baking), Woolworth's, and the stately courthouse where Grandpa Paisley had been a judge. Then the bus chugged back up the hill. We got off at Mackey's confectioners for strawberry ice cream cones and then walked the rest of the way home.

Even when I grew up and moved to new cities, I loved riding mass transit—to get a tour of the city, to feel like a local. I rode the yellow trolleys in Pittsburgh in college. A TWA stewardess based in San Francisco, I went blocks out of my way to hop on the clanging cable cars. It was fun being with all those other people, wondering what their lives were like and watching the world go by.

In 1964 I moved to New York City. For years I got around by walking or dashing underground to take the subway. But I sometimes felt small on the sidewalk amid the skyscrapers or a bit cut off in the underground tunnels. One drizzly day, as I lugged a shoulder bag full of manuscripts to work, I saw the bus coming. The bus! I climbed aboard. Instantly I felt at home again.

And so began my mornings on the No. 5 bus. I'd leave my

apartment and wait near a pretty park along the Hudson for the bus to come. I'd get a seat if I was lucky. Or I'd hold tight to the overhead bar as the bus swept down Broadway, passing Harriet's Heavenly Nail Salon, glorious Lincoln Center, the American Bible Society building, and a place above a bodega where, according to the sign, you could "Learn to Scuba Dive" right in the middle of Manhattan. Finally we reached my stop on Thirty-third Street and Fifth Avenue, right next to the Empire State Building.

From the bus window, I've seen Amish women in sunbonnets, Hasidic men wearing broad-brimmed hats, a gaggle of girls whose earrings swung like wind chimes, and a boy walking five dogs tugging him in different directions. There have been schoolkids break-dancing, truckloads of bagels being delivered, and Mel Gibson making a movie. What a difference from Steubenville, Ohio!

The passengers have been a cross section of ages, ethnicities, and nationalities. They read newspapers, novels, guidebooks, and Bibles in half a dozen languages. Conversations rise and fall like music. Once a woman passed around a jar containing her latest kidney stone. On a winter morning the trip turned into a Seinfeld episode when a disgruntled passenger, a stubborn driver, and an annoyed policeman exchanged words, and the bus was declared "under arrest." I've even seen a Chihuahua jump out of a man's shirt.

One day the bus got stuck in traffic, and I glanced at my watch, a headache rising. *Dear God, I'm going to be late. Help me calm down.* That's when I looked out the window and saw a disheveled man pointing at our bus. "Look at all those normal people rushing to go to work!" he shouted. "They must be crazy!" I laughed out loud.

Another time I wondered how I'd juggle a visit to a sick

friend, a family wedding, and a speech at a women's retreat. Then I saw a panel in the bus ceiling that said, "Push up for ventilation." I took some deep breaths and settled down. A few weeks later my anxieties kicked in again as I struggled to draft an article. On came a recorded warning about pickpockets: "Be alert for staged distractions." Aha! That's what my mind was doing, staging its own distractions of worry and doubt. I refocused and kept writing.

But the best help has come from other people on the bus. One morning last spring I was in a snit because—readers, you can choose a reason—I slept through the alarm/couldn't find a clean blouse/remembered that I forgot to clean the litter box. The bus pulled up and the door whooshed open to reveal a beaming driver. "Why are you lookin' so down?" he boomed. "Come aboard! Be happy! The world's a wonderful place!" His greeting changed my whole attitude.

Last July I sat by the window blinking back tears after having my twenty-year-old cat, Lucy, euthanized. *Holy Spirit, I could use some help here.* A few blocks later a woman who'd once lived in my apartment building boarded the bus. "How are you?" Ann asked as she took the seat beside me.

"I had to have Lucy put to sleep yesterday. How's your dog, Toby?"

"Toby's in pretty bad shape," she said. "I think I'll have to do the same thing soon." We told stories about the animals we loved, patted each other's arms, and wiped the tears from our eyes. "This is what Jewish people do when they sit shivah," Ann said. "After the death of a loved one, we tell stories and comfort each other. You and I are sitting shivah right here on the bus."

I thanked her. "Being with you today is an answer to prayer," I said.

An answer to prayer. How many times a ride on the No. 5 bus had proven to be just that! All I had to do was pay attention to the answers all around me.

Last September 11 on my way to work traffic came to a complete standstill. Suddenly a woman wearing a headset gasped. "The radio says a plane crashed into the World Trade Center," she said. *Give strength and courage to those in danger,* I prayed.

The next few days the bus was quiet, shock and sadness on everyone's face. A caretaker kissed the cheek of an elderly woman in a wheelchair. A father reassured his daughter, his big hand cradling her small fingers. The driver said, "We all have to watch out for each other." I thought of the words of Jesus: *I will not leave you comfortless.*

That comfort stayed with me in the following weeks as passengers started to chat and laugh again, pens came out for crossword puzzles, and a baby hurled a rubber alligator while a man in a business suit returned it to her again and again.

These are the people who give me the heart to go on. They are the answers to my prayers. Answers that surround us every day when we become part of a community. For me that community can be as close as a ride on the No. 5 bus.

You are best to yourself when you are good to others.
—AUTHOR UNKNOWN

THE CAT WHO WOULDN'T COME OUT

CHRISTINE CONTI

When my next-door neighbor Sally begged me to take in a homeless cat, I was almost ready to end our friendship.

I was tired of flea-ridden animals with sad eyes and dirty coats. I had adopted, rehabilitated, and found homes for more of them than I cared to admit. I was just getting reacquainted with my own neglected cats and planning my return to daily prayer and Bible study when Sally showed up. She sat on my couch staring apologetically into her coffee cup as she gave me the details.

The cat had been cherished by the Hetricks, an elderly couple who lived down the street. The wife had entered a nursing home, and now her husband was sick and needed care himself. They had no children, just some in-laws who were allergic to cats and were thinking of putting the pet in a shelter.

"But people don't go to shelters looking for twelve-year-old cats," Sally said. "She'll be destroyed. I'd take her, but my cat Maggie hates other cats. Yours, though, are used to strangers."

"Well, sort of," I said. It had only taken a week for them to emerge from under the bed when I brought the last stray home. I smiled at Sally and thought about moving.

"Her name's Ebony," she said. "She's black with a splash of white on her chest."

"Oh, all right," I said, as if this were the deciding point.

"I'll take her, but just till I find her another home." Actually, it was the plight of the elderly couple that moved me: I often wondered who would care for my animals if I couldn't.

Sally and I made plans to meet the cat-allergic in-laws who were temporarily caring for the Hetricks' house and Ebony. Sally left, and I went upstairs to prepare an unused bedroom—cats need their own space. The room was empty except for some rolled-up carpets and boxes of winter clothes. Muttering under my breath about yet another burden, I arranged a jumble of boxes, plastic milk crates, and old blankets to provide a variety of hiding and sleeping places. Then I grabbed a cat carrier and was off.

When I got to the Hetricks' house, the in-laws told me Ebony had been hiding in the cellar for as long as they had been there—about two weeks. Uh-oh, I thought, not a friendly cat.

Sally and I were able to extract a cat-shaped mop of long black fur from underneath the furnace, get her into the cat carrier, and release her into my upstairs room. She immediately dashed for a milk crate behind the pile of rolled-up carpets. My cats, Damian and Mookie, were furious and alternated between rushing the pile, hissing furiously, and beating a terrified retreat to cower in my room.

Frankly I didn't feel much differently; a new cat meant more food, litter, and visits to the vet. What had I been thinking?

My resentment softened when I unpacked her things. There was a well-worn, often-repaired toy mouse, a carpet in the shape and colors of a rainbow, and, most heart-tugging of all, a handmade label on her food canister which read in fancy, crayoned letters: "Ebony—Our Pride and Joy!" All my previous refugees had been unwanted and uncared for; this was a cat that had been loved.

It wasn't an easy few weeks. Ebony was so unfriendly. Except for the necessities, which she accomplished at night, Ebony wouldn't leave her crate behind the carpet, much less her room. How was I going to find a home for her? What sort of ads and signs could I write? "Aging, unfriendly cat needs loving home"?

I bought toys, tried homeopathic remedies, positioned a mirror on the floor by the doorway so she could see from inside her room that the hall outside was cat-free. . . . Nothing worked. Mookie and Damian didn't help either—they got over their fear and hostility but avoided her room. My vet told me that Ebony might come out in a few months, or she just might stay in that room for the rest of her life. I prayed for inspiration, and an old saying popped to mind: If the mountain wouldn't come to me, I would go to the mountain. Perhaps if I spent some time in the room with Ebony every day, she'd get used to me and come out.

At first I didn't know what I'd do in there. There was no television, radio, stereo, or sewing machine, not even a chair. I'll take in a book, I thought. The Bible.

I brought a lamp into the room and perched it on a box. Then I sat next to it on the floor, resting my back against the pile of rolled-up carpets. I twisted around and reached in to Ebony's carton to pet her and say hello. Then I turned back and read Scripture and prayed. It was wonderfully peaceful, and I stayed much longer than I had intended.

The next day and the next day and the next, right after breakfast, I had my quiet time in what I had come to think of as Ebony's room. Soon it was a firm habit. I became so absorbed in reading and praying that, one day, when Ebony crept out of hiding and sat cautiously a few feet away from me, I barely noticed. When I finished my prayers, I got my first really good look at her: a solidly built, long-haired black cat with springy whiskers and a dusting of white on her chest.

It wasn't long before Ebony jumped out of her box when I appeared, purred, rolled around happily, and curled up next to me while I prayed and read. One day I came across the admonition: *"And let us not be weary in well doing: for in due season we shall reap, if we faint not"* (Galatians 6:9). I looked at Ebony, whom I had so resented, who had made me feel so weary, and thanked God for sending her and restoring to me my quiet time.

That was three months ago. Ebony is now a permanent part of my home—though she isn't out of her room yet. But even if she never ventures into the rest of the house, I will continue to go to her. My visits there are the high point of my day—not just because of the time I spend with Ebony, though I've come to dote on her, but because of the time I spend with God.

The love of our neighbor is the only door
out of the dungeon of self.
—GEORGE MACDONALD

NEVER FAR FROM FAMILY

PAT EGAN DEXTER

*M*y dog, Balaam, put her chin on my knee and eyed me expectantly. "Want to go for a walk, girl?" I asked. Immediately she circled and pranced. I held her still long enough to snap on her leash and then stepped out into the fresh air. It was a clear, hot August morning. Neighborhood sprinklers already chugged away, irrigating the southwestern desert lawns. Sunlight glinted off the leaves of the lemon and orange trees.

I opened the wrought-iron gate in the wall that surrounded my front yard, and out we trotted. Early morning walks always invigorated me. Or at least they used to. Lately I'd been fighting a nagging sense of loneliness and fear that I always seemed to wake up with. I knew it was because my youngest son, David —the last of my children to still live in the area—had recently moved away.

I was thrilled about my son's new job and the exciting prospects it held for him, his wife, and their three children. But on this particular day the reality of their departure—and the feeling of being all alone—hit me full force. My husband, Ralph, had died two years earlier. My closest family at the moment was Balaam, a black Labrador mix I'd found in a shelter and named after an Old Testament prophet.

Balaam bounded off with her usual energy and I had to move fast to keep up. I nodded to two young men cutting hedges and trimming grass on a neighbor's lawn, then moved on past my friend Dorothy's house. *She's lucky*, I thought. *She's got family close by.* It occurred to me I could stop in and chat with her about how I was feeling, but I dismissed the urge. I don't want to burden her with my problems.

Balaam trotted off toward a fig tree, wrapped her leash around the trunk, and gave a yip. "Don't worry, girl. I'll take care of you," I said, but as I fumbled to free her, the thought came loud and clear: *Who will take care of me if I get tangled up?* My mind raced with woeful scenarios—a bad case of the flu, a flat tire in the middle of nowhere, a gas leak, emergency surgery. Step by step, scare by scare, my apprehension intensified.

By then Balaam and I had spent forty minutes circling the neighborhood. Once we got back to our street, I didn't even glance at Dorothy's house to see if her door was open or acknowledge the two young gardeners who were now hoisting their lawn equipment into a blue pickup truck. I just wanted to go back inside and brood. I was several feet from my front gate when I stumbled on a raised area in the walk. I fell down and landed hard on the cement. Balaam's leash flew out of my hand. My right arm had smashed into the pavement and my head had grazed the wall. As I lay there stunned, the young men left their pickup and raced toward me.

"Señora," one of them called, "are you all right?"

As they approached, Balaam growled, her neck fur standing on end. She jumped up to protect me. "Girl, it's okay," I murmured, putting out my hand.

The young men stopped, afraid of the dog. One spoke Spanish to the other, who quickly translated. "He wants to know if we should call 911."

I wriggled my legs to see if there was any real damage.

None. "I'm okay. I live here." I gestured toward my house. "If I can get inside, I'll be fine."

Now that she was sure the men meant me no harm, Balaam stopped growling and backed away. They eased me to my feet, then watched with concern as I gingerly moved about.

"Can we call your family?" one asked.

"I don't have family," I said. "Nada."

"No *familia?*"

I shook my head again. "Not here, anyway." They looked puzzled, then saddened. One on each side, the men guided me into the house, where they eased me onto a chair beside the telephone. They offered to drive me to the hospital.

"Thank you, no," I said. Then as an afterthought I reached for my purse nearby. "Let me give you something for helping me," I told them.

"No, no." They both were emphatic. "You could have been our mother," one said. "We were glad to help. We are all *familia.*" They asked once again if I was sure I'd be okay and if there were anyone they could contact. I assured them I was fine and sent them on their way.

After a few minutes, I checked myself in the mirror. I had blue-purple bruises on my arm and knees and a scrape on my forehead, but other than that I wasn't seriously injured. The pain was almost gone, but what lingered just as forcefully were the young men's words: "We are all *familia.*"

I thought about it and realized family isn't just spouses and children and cousins and aunts. It's my neighbors, my community, the people I pass on the street. The mailman, who makes sure my mail is taken care of and welcomes me home when I get back from a trip. And Rosie, the cashier at the grocery store who asks how I'm doing and points out items on sale. There's the

Bemis family, who live next door and whose daughter Makenzie has watched Balaam on occasion. In my mind I listed name after name of people at church who had picked up prescriptions for me or called with requests for the prayer chain; they were definitely part of my family. And then there was the kindness of strangers, sometimes unexpected but welcome nonetheless, people ready to rush to pick you up when you took a tumble, like the two young gardeners. All of us belong to the family of God.

I picked up the phone and called my neighbor. "Hi, Dorothy," I said. "I tripped on the pavement and had a spill. No serious damage done but I'm a little shaken up. Would you mind coming over and having tea with me later?"

Dorothy showed up as soon as she could. I greeted her as *familia.*

Many individuals have, like uncut diamonds, shining qualities beneath a rough exterior.

—Juvenal

Unlikely Friendship

Marion Bond West

I first saw Patty at a yard sale at the church where my husband, Gene, was the new minister and I was just getting acquainted with the folks in the congregation. I was about to go say hello to her when someone whispered to me, "That's Patty Anderson. Hasn't been to services in twenty years."

I studied Patty covertly. She was about forty, with pretty blond hair. She didn't mingle or chitchat. She stood by herself, arms folded, quietly taking in everything.

"Just leave her be," my informant advised.

I nodded. Patty looked unapproachable anyway. Her manner, even her height—nearly six feet—seemed off-putting. But then I heard another whisper, one that seemed to come from inside: *Go over and visit with Patty. Pray for her.*

Pray for her? Patty wouldn't like me or my prayers. Not if she felt uncomfortable with the church. But, oddly, that's where I saw her next. Her parents, who were regular churchgoers, held a family reunion in the fellowship hall and invited Gene and me.

When I spotted Patty, I again felt an inner urging: *Get to know her.* And again I ignored it. She had left the church and I was the minister's wife —what could we have in common?

One Saturday morning not long after, I stopped by the church and nearly tripped over a small, bedraggled dog huddled in the doorway. I scooped him up in my arms. He wasn't wearing any tags. There was no way on earth Gene would let me bring home yet another stray, but I couldn't leave the poor pup to fend for himself.

Just then a man from our congregation drove past. He saw me with the dog and pulled into the parking lot. "Try Patty Anderson," he suggested. "She lives just across the road, and she loves animals."

I didn't want to impose on Patty, but I didn't have any other options. I looked up her number and dialed, almost hoping no one would answer. When someone picked up, I mumbled, "Um . . . I need to speak with Patty, please."

"This is Patty."

"Hi, Patty. You don't know me. I'm Marion."

"I know who you are." Her voice was unhurried. "You're the new minister's wife. I saw you at the yard sale and our family reunion."

Where I never even bothered to say hello, I thought guiltily. "I'm so sorry to bother you. I'm at the church." I could hear myself babbling, as I always do when I'm nervous. "There's an abandoned dog here, and I wondered if . . ."

"Stay put. I'll be right over." When Patty came in she headed straight for the dog. I watched, grateful we wouldn't have to make small talk, as she bent down and spoke directly to him. "Hey, little guy," Patty murmured, her serious expression melting. "Looks like you need a good meal. How about coming home with me?" The dog just about wagged his tail off. "I'll take him," she said, and gathered him in her arms. "Thanks for calling." Then she was out the door.

The next week I stopped by her house to check on the dog. But really, I'll admit, I was curious about Patty. She answered the door, a bit surprised, then invited me in.

Right on the living-room sofa sat the dog, head held high as though he understood he belonged. "I named him Shorty," Patty volunteered. I nodded and squeezed out a smile.

Then I noticed the cats—well-fed, we've-got-it-made-and-we-know-it cats. "Oh, your cats! They're beautiful!"

Patty introduced them one by one: Elvis, Wee Wee, Doodlebug, and Sally. Then her voice softened. "They were all starving or hurt when I found them. I owe my soul and all my future income to the wonderful vets here in Monroe. Dr. Wall and Dr. Gross have even made house calls."

This time the smile I gave her was genuine. Patty was as crazy about animals as I was! I couldn't help but feel a little less intimidated. We started calling each other to talk about our pets or an abandoned dog one of us was trying to find a home for. Patty told me about a malnourished black cat she had found in the woods behind her house. Day after day she had watched him devour the food she left for him and then dash back into his hiding place. "I named him Kitty Boy," she said. "Do you think he'll ever let me get close to him, Marion?"

"He will," I said. "I'm certain of it."

We began talking to each other about practically everything. Hairstyles, our favorite recipes, her obsession with car races (she had even driven her vintage '67 Chevelle to Indianapolis to watch a week of drag races—alone!), our husbands, things we had done (or hadn't) that we regretted. One day I confessed, "I should have visited with you at the yard sale. People said—"

"You don't have to explain," Patty interrupted, stroking Kitty Boy's thick fur. Eyes shut in contentment, he lay at her feet and purred like a tiny vacuum cleaner. "When I first saw you I knew one day we'd be friends."

Patty was down-to-earth and straightforward. I admired the way she wasn't afraid to say what she thought. I discovered I didn't like Patty just a little; I liked her a lot. When she confided in me about her health problems—she suffered debilitating pain, from her hands to her back to her feet, and doctors seemed baffled as to its cause—I knew she felt the same way about me.

As we became closer I pictured Patty coming to church again—with me. We would walk in together and sit close to the front, sharing a hymnal. She would believe exactly as I did. Privately I prayed for Patty, for her pain to subside and her mysterious ailment to be healed, but that was the one thing I didn't feel comfortable mentioning to her.

Then she had to go in for surgery. Walking down the hospital corridor to her room, I felt as awkward as I had the first time I went to her house. When I visited church members in the hospital I prayed with them and read Scripture. But with Patty, I wasn't sure what I was supposed to do.

I knocked on the door. No answer. I pushed it open gently and tiptoed in. Patty lay in bed looking crumpled and pale. When I saw the pain and fear in her eyes, I wondered, *Will I be able to help her?* Right away her mouth turned up at the corners, and she patted the bed for me to sit. I sat as close as I could and reached for her hand, trying to think of the right words to say.

My thoughts were interrupted by the insistent urge that I had tried to ignore for months: *Pray for Patty.* But what if she rejected my prayers? What if she rejected me?

Pray for Patty. Now. She needs you.

I took a deep breath. "Patty, can I pray for you?" I asked hesitantly. She nodded. I closed my eyes and petitioned God to heal my friend. The words rolled off my tongue effortlessly, as if they came not from me, but rather, through me.

An extraordinary force flowed from me to Patty: love. Stronger at that instant than any love I had ever felt for her—or for anyone. All-encompassing love so intense it could have come only from God.

I opened my eyes. "Thank you," Patty whispered.

Praying for Patty never felt uncomfortable after that. While she was recuperating at home I visited and prayed with her there. It seemed as if her cats and Shorty were all part of our impromptu prayer circle. She sent me a note thanking me for seeing her in the hospital. We had exchanged plenty of cards before, but now for the first time she ended with, "I love you. Patty." I read those words over and over, remembering how I had stubbornly resisted God's prompting because I was afraid Patty wouldn't want anything to do with me. As always, God had known better than I, and He brought Patty and me together.

Seven years have passed since we met. Patty and I are as close as ever. She hasn't come to church with me, and there are still some things we don't talk about. But I have learned to trust that we were meant to be friends. We need each other. We love each other. Isn't that what really matters?

The noblest service comes from unseen hands.
—OLIVER WENDELL HOLMES

THE CLUES IN THE QUILT

DRU QUARLES

J was browsing in a flea market near my home that spring afternoon in 1997 when I turned and saw it—an old quilt draped over a screen. Its large white squares were framed with soft pink cotton. But it was the contents of each square that made me stop and look more closely. Stiches of black thread radiated from the center of each square like spokes on a wheel. And names were embroidered between the spokes—an entire community, it seemed, of people named Armalee and Madie and Ruby and Errol.

"Three-hundred and seventy-six of 'em, lady," the dealer said. "I counted. The guy I bought it from said it came from somewhere in north Georgia. It's probably fifty years old."

The dealer spread the quilt on a table so I could have a better look. I continued to read, drawn into a whole new world of people who, I had a feeling, were as interesting as their names—Chester Wester, Flossie Foster, Dr. John Walker . . . *A doctor like me,* I thought. In my mind I pictured a kindly general practitioner who had helped generations of the same family enter and leave the world. A doctor unlike me. I worked in a technology-driven world where everything was state of the art; and instead of a simple black bag, a few trusty medicines, and a lot of reassurance, we had a galaxy of "miracle" drugs and HMOs.

The quilt was a relic from a more leisurely time. *A better one,* I thought wistfully. From the variations in stitches and style, I could tell many different hands had been involved. "A friendship quilt," I said. I knew that people years ago often got together to sew their names on a quilt as a special gift or project. My fingers stroked the cotton worn soft from wear and the nubby lines of embroidery. "This would really mean something to the families of the people who stitched it," I mused.

"Might," the dealer said. "If you could just find 'em."

Well, maybe I'd try. Impulsively, I bought the quilt. At home, I showed it to my husband, then spread it like a coverlet on the four-poster bed in our guest room. I couldn't get the quilt out of my mind. When I came home at night, tired after a long day of seeing patients, reading test results, and keeping up with endless paperwork, I flopped on the bed and traced the embroidered names with my fingers. Jane Corn, Pearl Ackle, Annie Moon. Where had they lived? Where had the quilt come from? And what about Dr. Walker? Unlike me, constantly filling out referral forms, he'd probably been in every home in the community and had known the intimate details of the daily lives of his patients.

At work I checked serum electrolytes, marked charts for fluid intakes and outputs, and ran electronic inquiries to see if a patient's insurance would cover a lung scan. I sometimes spent more time at my computer than with patients. I came home bushed, but somehow I always ended up studying that quilt again. In places the thread was twisted or knotted to cover mistakes. Clearly, some of the ladies hadn't been skilled seamstresses. But that hadn't kept them from making their contribution. And look—on one of the squares was stitched Kate and Mike and a question mark. Did that mean Kate and Mike had been expecting a new baby? I smiled at the possibility.

It was as if I had a roomful of grandmothers whispering stories of bygone days. As I fell under the quilt's spell, I strongly felt the need to find out where this special blanket had come from and who might want it back.

In July my parents and sister, Holly, came from Kentucky to visit me. Dad's an amateur genealogist who had traced our family tree. Going to courthouses and libraries, he'd gone back generations, listing our ancestors on a length of wallpaper! Now that he'd retired, I asked Dad if he'd be interested in tracing the original owners of the quilt. After sleeping under the pink and white cover with the spiderweb of names, he too was intrigued.

"This seems like a long shot, but we'll give it a go," Dad said. "Let's pick out twenty of the more unusual names. Maybe we can track them down through government records." Then my sister came up with another idea: "Why don't we put the names on the Internet?"

The Internet? It hadn't occurred to me that a search back through history could take place on the modern information superhighway. "Okay, Dad," I said. "Go for it."

My family went home to Kentucky and went to work, logging on to search engines and databases on the World Wide Web that go through thousands of phone-book type listings in seconds. On his computer, Dad went through towns, states, even merchandising lists. He typed in names from the quilt, then clicked on "Search." For Pearl Ackle. For Annie Moon.

Dad kept me posted on his progress. Chester Wester? Nothing. Flossie Foster? Nothing. He'd hoped that someone on the Internet would recognize names like Joyce Lucky Zagaroli, Carter Harold Butterworth, Junior Motes, and Beverly Snook. But there were no matches or responses. Were any of these people still alive? Any of their families?

Then one day I picked up the phone to hear Dad exclaim, "I did a search on the Internet, and I've found a Jane Corn! I've got her number in Dahlonega, Georgia."

It turned out, though, that this Jane Corn knew nothing about the quilt. "But," she said, "it sounds like something my mother and grandmother might have helped embroider at church." At church! Of course, why hadn't we thought of that? She gave us the names of the two churches they had attended— Elizabeth Baptist and Welcome Grove Baptist, both in Marietta, Georgia.

But Dad's phone calls there produced no answers. "No one at those churches knows anything about the quilt," Dad reported. I sighed, disappointed. "But," he added, "I did learn that they shared the same minister, Ralph Foster. And one of the people I spoke to remembered the reverend had pastored another church on the outskirts of town—Chattahoochee Baptist."

The next day Dad called me, nearly shouting with excitement. "I telephoned the church clerk at Chattahoochee," he said. "The person who answered the phone sounded pretty young and didn't recognize any of the names. But she called their church historian, Jeanette Samples, who's seventy-six. 'Of course I know those people!' she said. 'We all made that quilt over forty years ago. We stitched on our names and gave it to Reverend Foster when he answered the call to another church and moved away.'" They'd later learned that when Rev. Ralph Foster died, the quilt had somehow been sold—never, they thought, to be seen again.

It was time for the quilt to go home. On a beautiful Sunday morning in November 1997, my parents and husband and I drove 200 miles to Chattahoochee Baptist Church to present the quilt to the congregation.

The quiet little clapboard country church I had pictured in my mind turned out to be a modern brick building on a six-lane highway. But the people were as welcoming and friendly as any old-fashioned congregation in my dreams. At the service Dad and I presented the quilt. When Jeanette Samples got up to accept it, her voice quivered. "This is such a great joy," she said. "There are so many sweet names on here, names of folks who've gone on before us."

Jeanette gave me a hug, warm and soft like the quilt. Then we unfolded it and held it up so everyone could see. Jeanette's eyes filled with tears as her fingers closed on the square that she had embroidered so long ago with the names of her own family.

After the service, people crowded around, looking for the names of relatives or others they knew. Jeanette told me all she could remember about Annie Moon, Flossie Foster and others.

And what about Dr. Walker? Jeanette wasn't sure what had happened to him. But as we strolled around the church, I was reminded of something a doctor had told me when I was a third-year medical student: "The person who your granny thinks is the best doctor didn't go to Johns Hopkins or do cutting-edge research. The best doctor to her is the one who asked for her apple pie recipe and wanted to see a picture of her grandchildren."

We wandered into the small graveyard out back where I saw Chester Wester's tombstone, along with those of others whose names had become so dear to me. As Jeanette shared the stories, I felt a sense of continuity and community, an unbroken thread of joys and sorrows and laughter and prayers, running throughout time.

That's something that will never change. People need to feel connected to one another, and whether it's through a friendship quilt or the Internet, God will find a way to bring us together.

Our Friends Above

There is no wilderness like a life without friends.
—BALTASAR GRACIÁN Y MORALES

OH, TO HAVE A FRIEND

HELEN GRACE LESCHEID

*F*orty years ago as a lonely immigrant girl in Canada, I had an experience so hard to describe that it took me many years even to try. Yet the story needs to be told, for it points up how intimately God knows His children.

That October day in 1952 as I listened to the lunchtime chatter in my high school homeroom, the ache in my throat made it hard to swallow my meal of dark rye bread. *Won't I ever belong?*

I was fifteen. Two years earlier I'd entered Lord Tweedsmuir High in Surrey, British Columbia, a frightened newcomer from Germany. Shy and awkward anyway, I'd been too ashamed of my limited English to reply when someone spoke to me.

As the months went by, my English improved but my sense of belonging did not. Everything about me was different from these outgoing Canadian girls—my accent, my hand-me-down clothes, my thick blond braids (too beautiful to cut, my mother said, when I pleaded that all the other girls wore their hair short). Even the lunch I brought from home: My classmates brought sandwiches on thin-sliced white bread; I had thick black rye and jam. I was the odd one, the outsider. In two years I'd made not a single friend.

I stuffed my uneaten lunch back inside my desk and fled from the happy babble of the classroom. Through crowded halls I pushed my way to the library. Books at least were usually my friends but not that day. As I glanced up from reading, I saw through the window an ordinary scene. Two girls sat on the grass, heads together, talking. Such longing rose inside me that I knew I was going to cry. Oh, to have a friend, just one friend with whom I could sit and talk that way!

I escaped from the library and dodged into the bathroom where I could lock the door and let the tears come. "Lord Jesus, I'm so lonely!" To talk to Jesus was natural to me; I'd been taught that He cared for each of us personally. I'd gaze at paintings of Him, thinking how friendly He looked, how I'd have told Him anything if I'd lived back then.

After school I stood as usual at the bus stop on the fringe of a knot of schoolmates. One of the girls turned to me. "Helen, are you going to the school dance on Friday?" I shook my head no. "Why don't you come?" she coaxed.

I shut my eyes against a memory. . . . At the last dance I'd stood on the sidelines for what seemed hours. At last a boy walked up to me, but what he did was yank one of my braids. Everyone had laughed. No, I'd never put myself through that again! The girl beside me fell silent, then turned back to the others.

I mounted the big yellow bus and scanned it for a seat by the window, where I could keep from meeting people's eyes. But the window seats were taken. I slumped down beside a girl who smiled at me. *She's friendly,* I thought. *I'd like to say something friendly to her.* I was too tongue-tied; throughout the half-hour ride I said not a word.

Close to tears again, I stumbled off the bus and hurried into the old farmhouse. As usual, our rented house was empty. Mother, who'd been widowed in World War II, worked up to ten hours in the vegetable fields each day to support herself and us four children. Come to think of it, my younger sisters and brother seemed to have no trouble making friends in our new country. They were probably off playing with the neighbor's kids at this very moment. It was me; something was terribly wrong with me.

Dropping my books on the kitchen table, I ran into the bedroom, slammed the door shut, and fell across the bed. My body, so flat and long and lanky, shook with sobs.

I sat up abruptly. Someone else was in the room! Hastily wiping my eyes I looked around. Nobody. But someone was here. I could feel it.

Not someone . . . Someone. There was an aura in that little room I could almost touch. Love such as I'd never felt before filled the space all around me. "Jesus," I whispered, "is that You?"

He answered, not with an audible voice, but with a love so tangible I felt hugged. Although I saw nothing physical, an image burned itself into my mind: a friendly face with smiling eyes, so vivid that even today forty years later I see them still. Eyes that danced and seemed to say, "You know what? I like you! You're my special friend!"

As I sat there on my bed, the glorious, gracious words kept coming: "Have you forgotten that you belong to Me? I will never leave you or forsake you. I'm here with you now and will always be with you. Don't be ashamed! I love you just as you are."

For a long time I sat there basking in love beyond my conceiving, hearing those words of unconditional acceptance. When my family came home, they found me humming as I prepared supper.

The next morning I opened my eyes to find the joyful Presence still filling the room, as though He'd waited for me to wake up so we could start the day together. When I boarded the yellow bus, He did too.

During class it was as though He were standing beside my desk. We did math problems together. We wrote essays together. Even in gym class, which I'd always dreaded, I could feel Him running beside me.

At lunch break that day, one of my classmates asked me if I would help her with a problem. She hadn't understood the teacher and felt sure I had. Wondering why she'd singled me out, yet thrilled that somebody had, I slid over and made room for her at my desk, not even trying to hide my chunk of bread.

Later at the bus stop, I stood with the familiar cluster of teens. My Friend whispered, "Aren't they a great bunch of kids? I also love them dearly." I turned to stare at them with new appreciation. Friendly eyes met mine. Later that week some girls invited me to join the glee club and I eagerly accepted.

The fact that my peers now wanted to be with me never ceased to amaze me. One day one of my sisters hinted at the reason. "Helen, what's happened to you? You're always so happy now!" I looked at her in surprise. True, I was supremely happy, but I hadn't been aware it showed.

For three glorious months my Friend and I walked in this indescribable companionship. I had never felt so completely believed in and understood. He was always smiling at me, a big smile of delight and approval; and it was impossible not to smile back at the world around me. Every morning when I got up, He was there. All day He walked beside me. In the evening my last awareness was of Him.

Then one dreadful morning I awoke to an empty room. The joyful Presence was gone. Panic seized me. "Jesus!" I cried. Silence. I must have sinned in some terrible way. Frantically I searched my conscience. I confessed every sin I could recall and begged Him to forgive my unknown ones. But the almost palpable sense of His presence did not return.

Grief-stricken, I opened my Bible. Where were those words Jesus had spoken to me three months before, right in this room? I found them in the thirteenth chapter of Hebrews: "He hath said, 'I will never leave thee, nor forsake thee.'"

I saw the words; I believed the words. But I did not feel them—not the way I had before. Slowly I repeated the words, "I will never leave thee, nor forsake thee."

"Jesus, did you say never so that I might know today that You are still with me even though I don't feel You?" I whispered. This glimmer of hope in time became a growing reality: No matter how I feel, Jesus is always with me. His love and acceptance are a fact independent of my moods and feelings.

It was only much later that I understood the double gift Jesus gave to a clumsy immigrant girl. He came as a tangible Presence to assure me of my value in His sight and to show me the value of friendship. Then He withdrew this special feeling. "You will find Me in My written Word," He seemed to be saying, "and in so many different ways." He stepped a little distance back, to make room for faith and character to grow. Isn't that what a best friend would do?

The impulse of love that leads us to the doorway
of a friend is the voice of God within.
—AGNES SANFORD

A LITTLE PATCH OF GREEN

JOAN WALSH ANGLUND

*P*eople tell me they like my books because they're hopeful and heartening. But, strangely enough, the first one came into being when I felt trapped in loneliness.

It was the autumn of 1956, and Bob and I had moved to New York City with our children, six-year-old Joy, and Todd, just two. We were hoping to find a receptive job market for our skills—Bob's as an actor and writer and mine as a freelance artist.

Almost as soon as we arrived, Bob had to go away on a six-week business trip and I was left alone in a new apartment in a strange city with two small children. I had always lived in a small, friendly suburb outside of Chicago. Now, in such unfamiliar surroundings, with no friends or family nearby, I felt overwhelmed. I "forgot to remember" what I'd been told all my life: God often brings change to us to help us grow.

When I was a little girl, it was my grandmother's faith that inspired me most. I loved to go to church with Nana. I sensed the peace she got from her trust in God's purpose. "He is in everything that happens to us, Joan," she assured me. "God always has a reason for the experiences and opportunities and abilities He gives us. You must use His gifts to grow, to give something back to life."

But to me, New York City didn't seem a bit hospitable to growth! After the neighborly surroundings I'd grown up with in Hinsdale, Illinois—the family homes, green streets, and gardens—the tall, gray buildings seemed bleak and cold. When I looked out of the windows of our apartment, all I could see were concrete, brick, and granite. Eventually I did spot a single "oasis." Small as a toy among the high-rising towers stood one little old-fashioned house with a yard that was actually covered with grass. In the yard were one small tree and one small boy playing by himself.

How sad! I thought. Just one little patch of green.

The fact that Bob's assignments often took him out of town added to my sense of isolation. And I was too busy with settling into my apartment, caring for Joy and Todd, and the usual homemaking routines to explore my new world and get acquainted. At least that's the excuse I gave myself.

But I did find odd moments to work in my sketchbook. I was especially fascinated with trying to capture the wonder and innocence of our children's faces, the soft, sweet curving of their features and heads.

The fall months passed and winter set in. With the new year came freezing weather—too cold to take Joy and Todd for outings. Since we didn't know anyone to visit or to invite in to play, the only alternative to our own four walls was the public library. There, in the whispering steam heat, we spent hour after hour looking at books.

As we walked home in the early-dark afternoons, I looked up longingly at the brightly lit windows in the tall buildings. So many lives surrounded us on all sides. Yet I was too unsure of myself to make friendly overtures.

Spring came at last. Again Bob had to be away. On one beautiful May morning, to cheer us all up, I took the children to a playground in the vicinity. After they'd busied themselves in a sandbox, I sat down on a bench and raised my face to the warmth of the sun. I could not feel it. I was so miserable, so lonely.

The air stirred softly. Joy and Todd glanced at me from time to time, then went on playing and chattering away, secure in the knowledge that I was nearby. I closed my eyes and, quite unexpectedly, three gentle, reassuring phrases floated through my mind:

I am not far away.

I am very, very near you.

I am never far away.

An utter stillness came over me. I had been thinking protectively of my children, but in my heart I knew those gracious words were meant for me. They had come from the Friend whose loving concern I'd learned to trust with Nana so long ago, the Friend who had always been close to me. In His constant company, I didn't need to be lonely!

Sunlight glowed on my cheeks and a feeling of gratitude filled my heart, gratitude for God's presence in my life and for all that He had given me: for Bob, so considerate and supportive; for our children; for our close, warm family; even for the "oasis" I looked at so often from my high window. I began to smile. *What a brave little patch of green,* I thought.

A few days later, the children and I walked past the little house with the green yard. Through the fence we could see the little boy playing with a ball. We stopped and I waved to him. He waved back and came closer, and then Joy said, "Hello! What's your name?" As we were talking, his mother came out of the house and joined us, and that was the way a new friendship began.

In the weeks that followed, I began to scribble down my thoughts—very simple thoughts—in an old steno pad. I wrote:

"Sometimes you don't know who are your friends. Sometimes they are there all the time, but you walk right past them and don't notice that they like you in a special way."

That's how I felt about the nearness of God in my life. Like the friendly people who lived and worked in my neighborhood, He was there all the time, waiting to be acknowledged.

One day Bob found the pad with my jottings. "Joan, this is like a little story. Why don't you illustrate it?"

I was puzzled. "Illustrate it? But it's not a book."

"I know you don't think of it as a book. But just try to draw pictures to fit your words."

And I did. I drew Joy and Todd. I drew the little boy who lived in the old-fashioned house. I drew his green yard and the tree that grew in it. I drew animals and birds and flowers—all the motifs I'd felt close to since childhood.

Not long after, without telling me, Bob took my words and pictures to a publishing house. Before he'd even come home, the telephone rang in our apartment. It was the editor Bob had spoken to. "Well, Mrs. Anglund," she said, "I think you have a book here."

"A book?" I echoed, dumbfounded.

"Why, yes, the book your husband left with me. The one you call *A Friend Is Someone Who Likes You.*"

For me, the fact that I'd done a book was not as important as the lesson I'd learned about Someone who loves us all. If you seek His friendship, you are sure to grow—no matter where you are.

Like that little patch of green.

Prayer—the very highest energy of which the mind is capable.
—SAMUEL TAYLOR COLERIDGE

A BLESSED FRIENDSHIP

PAMELA KENNEDY

I stood on the porch and waved good-bye as my friend, Linda, pulled out of the driveway. How I enjoyed her visits! As often as our schedules allowed, we carved out time to visit a local park, eat a bit of lunch, take in a movie, or just sit and talk. Together we shared ideas and experiences about decorating, dealing with our adult children, impending career changes, and family crises. We have always shared a comfortable, easy friendship devoid of competition or touchiness.

Too bad, I thought as I went inside, that there aren't more friendships like ours. Some people seem to want to be friends only when things are going badly or when they need something. Others want to be friends only when it's convenient or until someone more exciting or interesting comes along. As I picked up the empty cups and rinsed the lunch dishes, I flipped on the radio to a favorite station and hummed along. I was replacing the dishes on the shelves when the words to the radio hymn penetrated my thoughts: "What a friend we have in Jesus . . . "

It was an old and familiar sentiment. In fact, I recall my grandmother singing it when I was just a little girl. But because of my thoughts about my friendship with Linda, it was as if I heard the words for the first time. What struck me wasn't the realization of the Lord's friendship toward me but of how I reciprocated that friendship. What kind of a friend was I to Him?

My prayer time usually consisted of a few introductory

"thank you's" followed by a long litany of "pleases." Please help me get through this busy week. Please give me wisdom to know what to say. Please heal me of this illness quickly. Please watch over my loved ones. There was no time for listening and few questions that weren't related to my needs or wants. Somehow, in my relationship with my heavenly Father, I had become just the kind of friend I didn't like. When things were going well, I never stopped by for a chat. When the sun was shining, I was too busy for conversation. But let dark clouds gather at my horizon, let worry knock at my front door, and there I was on my knees asking for favors.

I know God wants us to come to Him with our problems and concerns. And I am certain He willingly helps us bear our burdens. But I wonder if He also longs for us to be close friends with Him, friends who can't wait to tell Him when something wonderful happens. Does His heart gladden when we pour out our joy to Him? As we marvel at a rainbow or a magnificent mountain or the delicate symmetry of a dragonfly, would He like to hear a word of appreciation? Is there a place in His heart that warms when we express our gratitude for the wonders of breath and heartbeat?

Near the end of His earthly life, when He spoke with His disciples, Jesus told them He would no longer call them servants but would call them His friends. Wasn't He telling us that too? He desires us to be friends who visit with Him at all times—friends who truly enjoy one another's company.

I turned off the radio and sat down at the kitchen table. I imagined Jesus sitting across from me, sharing a cup of coffee, spending time with me just like good friends do. A smile crept into the corners of my mouth as I recalled something Linda had shared. "Lord," I whispered softly, "wait till You hear what happened today."

Friendships form among people who strengthen one another.
—FRANKLIN OWEN

FLIGHT OF THE *MARY BETH*

NIKKI MITCHELL AND RHONDA MILES

*N*ikki Mitchell: Rhonda and I are so close it's hard for us to imagine a time we weren't a part of each other's lives. But every friendship, like every journey, has a beginning. Ours, fittingly, got its start at the little airport in Lebanon, Tennessee, east of Nashville.

I went out there one day in June 1996 to check on the secondhand Maule M-5 I'd just bought, a plane that pilots call a tail-dragger because it has a wheel in the back (rather than under the nose as with most aircraft), making it ideal for landing on rough terrain. Sure, the Maule had seen better days, but to me it was new and exciting. I didn't have much experience at the controls of that type of plane, and I was thrilled I'd soon be flying a single-engine tail-dragger. It would open up a new world to me, the way stories of the pioneers of aviation had when I was growing up. I'd already named the Maule *Mary Beth*, in memory of a friend who had loved hearing about those heroes of mine.

Not so fast, I reminded myself as I walked across the tarmac that summer afternoon. *Before you take her up, you need someone to show you the fine points of flying a tail-dragger.*

That's when Rhonda Miles walked by. I don't know whether it was her confidence or sense of purpose that got my attention, or the iron and the foot-long needle she was carrying, but something made me ask what she was up to. She told me she was patching the canvas fuselage of her 1946 J3 Cub, and I thought, *wow, this girl knows airplanes!*

Not just any airplanes, either. She had 3,800 hours of experience flying tail-draggers, vintage (like her's) and modern (like *Mary Beth*). Rhonda was a professional pilot. As soon as I found out she was an instructor to boot, I asked her about lessons.

Rhonda Miles: Our friendship took off from there. Quickly we moved beyond discussing the technical aspects of aviation to talking about anything and everything. About our jobs—Nikki is president of country-music star Waylon Jennings's company; I fly full-time for Cracker Barrel restaurants and part-time for Reba McEntire. About our travels—her interest in history had led her to Russia to research an elite, all-female squadron of World War II pilots; my taste for adventure had taken me to the jungles of a South Pacific island to search for the remains of a pilot from the same war.

As we talked about our families, we discovered both of us have flying in our blood. Nikki's father was a career Air Force man, and she was so enthralled by his stories that she got her pilot's license at age eighteen. My dad is a crop duster in Pine Bluff, Arkansas, and I grew up riding in his ag plane. Even after fourteen hours straight in that cramped cockpit, Dad couldn't wait to take to the air again. "C'mon, Toot," he'd say to me at night, "let's go look at the stars up close." I must be my dad made over again, because there's still nothing I love more than cruising the skies, anytime, anywhere.

Nikki: One afternoon as we were bringing *Mary Beth* in, I filled Rhonda in on an amazing achievement I'd learned about while doing my historical research. I told her about the three Russian women who, in 1938, took the *Rodina* where no plane had gone before—from Moscow to the southeastern tip of Siberia.

Right away I saw that Rhonda was fascinated. "The sixtieth anniversary of the flight is in two years," I said. "What if we commemorated it by retracing their route using *Mary Beth*? Is it possible?"

"Sure, we can do it!" Rhonda replied. We shook hands on it. Just like that, two months after we met, Rhonda and I became partners in an incredible dream.

Rhonda: And just like that, our dream pretty much became our lives. At the end of every workday I met Nikki at her office to plan our trip. In order to make the commemorative flight and return home, we'd have to circle the globe. We set July 4, 1998, as our takeoff date. That gave us less than two years to work out a mind-boggling number of details, such as arranging for food, lodging, and plane fuel along a route that included some of the most remote areas on earth and giving *Mary Beth* a complete overhaul so she could withstand the rigors of a 15,000-mile flight.

Night after night Nikki and I were at it till late, writing letters and making phone calls to try to raise interest in (and funds for) our project. We did plenty of praying too.

Nikki: So many people told us, "Forget it. Two women flying around the world in that little plane? You'll never pull it off." We got turned down more often than not. Yet amid all that seemed to go wrong, from time to time one extraordinary thing would go right and move us a step closer to realizing our dream.

For instance, the president of the Russian women aviators' association suggested that two of their pilots fly side by side with us to honor the *Rodina* and foster goodwill between nations. Rhonda and I were in awe: What started out as an adventure now had a higher purpose. Our dream was taking on a life of its own.

No one could move the lumbering Russian bureaucracy along, though. After we'd lined up sponsors and made arrangements for the rest of the trip, we were still waiting for the go-ahead from the Russian government on the commemorative route. In the spirit of international unity, we'd named our flight "A Bridge of Wings," but now those wings were having difficulty getting off the ground.

Rhonda: In the spring of 1998, while *Mary Beth* was being outfitted with her new engine, propeller, tail wheel, and navigation and communication systems, Nikki and I went to Moscow to meet with Russian aviation authorities to try to smooth out the problems.

So many people there were behind us, from the national aviation committee to local aeronautics clubs. Celebrations were already being planned for the beginning and end of the route. We hit it off immediately with Khalide Makaganova and Natalia "Natassia" Vinokourova, the Russian pilots who'd be flying with us. Their faces lit up when we talked about our flight, and for the first time it occurred to me that Nikki and I weren't the only ones who had hopes riding on "A Bridge of Wings." Khalide and Natassia were eager to map out the landing and fuel points across the vast stretch of Siberian forest and marsh; but they were afraid that with the shaky Russian economy, there was little chance they'd get funding for their part of the flight. Since we had backing from a number of sponsors, Nikki and I felt confident we could help cover our Russian friends' expenses also.

Nikki: Though we hadn't yet received formal permission, our meetings with the aviation authorities went well. Rhonda and I returned to Nashville feeling good about our prospects.

Then some major sponsors (including the company that

was to have supplied our fuel) pulled out. They said the Russian economy was too unpredictable, the whole flight was too risky, there was no way we'd succeed. Rhonda and I still believed in our dream, but how would we go on now?

Just as we were worrying about what to do, we got an e-mail from Khalide and Natassia. The mayor of Moscow had committed to funding their part of the flight! We couldn't let our friends down. We had to push on.

Rhonda: Nikki and I decided to go back to how we started—not with those big corporate sponsors, but with hard work, serious praying, and our faith in our dream. If it was the Lord's will for our journey to be, He would help us make it happen.

We sat down and began working out a bare-bones budget for the flight. When Nikki and I talked about the support we still had, we discovered that while we might not have had some of the things we'd planned, we had everything we needed: our families; our friends here and in Russia; our employers; our remaining sponsors—mostly small, family-run companies, folks who knew what it was like to be a single-engine tail-dragger in a world of jumbo jets; above all, we had each other, a bond that had become so strong we felt like sisters.

Nikki: Just three days before takeoff, the Russian aviation authorities granted us flight clearance. On July 4 at the Lebanon, Tennessee, airport, with our family and friends to see us off, Rhonda and I hit the sky.

We flew *Mary Beth* via the North Atlantic to Russia, with our mechanic, Mikey Priest, and his assistant, Rhonda's son Jeremy, traveling on commercial flights to meet us at various stops. I'd always thought land would rise abruptly from out of the ocean, but really it fades softly into view. Rhonda kept chuckling because I fell in love with almost every place we stopped—Greenland, Iceland, Norway.

Rhonda: I, too, was amazed by how many places could qualify for the most beautiful spot on God's earth—and by how friendly and helpful people were wherever we went. We got great tips on flying conditions and landing approaches from local pilots. Everyone wanted to invite us to dinner and hear about our trip.

Nikki: On July 23 we made it to St. Petersburg, where Khalide joined us. For the trip to Moscow, she and Rhonda took *Mary Beth*; and I flew in another plane. A lot of people came out to greet us when we landed on the grass runway at Tushino airfield outside Moscow—reporters, TV crews, Natassia, and other friends.

The next day we met with the female World War II pilots whose exploits I'd been researching. We walked into a room full of women with medals all over their dresses, women who'd risked their lives to defend their country. It was humbling to be in the company of my heroes.

Then, on July 27 we took off from Tushino airfield on the first leg of the route commemorating the *Rodina*, flying in formation, with *Mary Beth* flanked by two Antonov AN-2s (Natassia and I in one, Mikey and Jeremy and the support crew with military pilots in the other).

Four-and-a-half hours later we arrived in Kazan. A huge crowd was waiting by the hangar. Only when we shut down our engines did we realize a brass band was welcoming us with the "Chattanooga Choo Choo!"

Rhonda: Flying east the next day, I kept thinking about how my dad would love that part of Siberia. Gorgeous farm fields as far as the eye could see—an ag pilot's heaven.

Nikki: In every Russian village where we stopped, people welcomed us with open arms. I think the fact that we didn't have corporate logos on our flight suits helped them see we were all in this together to honor the achievements of our predecessors.

Rhonda: At a press conference later, we found out Russian air traffic controllers had planned to go on strike; but when they heard about our flight, they decided to postpone their action until they saw us safely through Russian airspace. Wow!

On August 5 we began the final leg of the commemorative route. We followed the coastline from Ayan to Osipenko, where the *Rodina*, running on fumes, had crash-landed in 1938. Our landing, like our whole trip, went unbelievably smoothly. If I hadn't been there with Nikki on that dusty airstrip, listening to the townspeople cheer, I would have thought it was all an impossible dream.

Nikki: After crossing the Bering Sea to Alaska and flying through the Northwest, Rhonda and I finally landed at the little airport in Lebanon, Tennessee, forty-nine days after we had first taken off. As soon as we climbed out of the *Mary Beth*, I bent and kissed the ground. When I looked up and saw everyone who'd turned out to welcome us home, I knew our journey was a dream—a dream God had made possible through all the people he'd brought into our lives.

Rhonda: . . . starting with each other. As Nikki and I stood on the tarmac hugging our family and friends, I remembered how we had first crossed paths in that same spot just two summers earlier. That day neither of us could've guessed we'd end up flying around the world together. Just goes to show you that when the Lord brings people together, there's no telling how far He'll take you!

Trust involves letting go and knowing God will catch you.
—JAMES C. DOBSON

HOPE IN THE NIGHT

DENISE BEARD

*I*n the spring of 1987, I was expecting my second child; I was due in late October. My husband, Bill, and I were living in a small two-family house, and we were hoping to rent something larger. Like all families, we had our worries, but nothing seemed overwhelming.

One April evening after washing the dishes and tucking in three-year-old Catherine, I went into the living room to kiss Bill good night then headed for bed. Lying there I kept thinking about our new baby. Would we have a boy or a girl? What would we name the child? And where could we put another crib? With a sigh I turned off the light. I started to roll over to go to sleep. All at once I realized I couldn't move. I was paralyzed. What was happening to me?

I opened my eyes wide. I became aware of two wispy forms floating over me, back and forth, back and forth, undulating in the air like smoke in a breeze. The room was filled with a brilliant white haze, so bright I could have read by it.

Don't be afraid. The words reached me as if the forms had conveyed the thought. Relaxing, I allowed the feeling of peace that filled the room to cover me. This state of bliss lasted several minutes, surging through me. Gradually, though, the beings drifted away and the white haze in the room cleared.

I cleared my throat and whispered, "Bill . . . " I wiggled my fingers and toes. I started to get up to tell Bill what had happened, then stopped, letting my head fall back. What would I say? How could I explain something I didn't understand?

I sensed something important was going to happen in our lives and I had only to remember the message: *Don't be afraid.* Afraid of what, I couldn't say. I drifted to sleep, my thoughts wrapped around the words.

A month later I was flipping through the local newspaper when my eye fell on a want ad for a church sexton. Bill and I had never belonged to a church, and I had no idea what the job might entail. But from the description I gathered it involved janitorial, handyman, and groundskeeping work. What really intrigued me, though, was the last line: "Apartment comes with the job."

Catching my enthusiasm, Bill applied for the position at St. Mark's Episcopal Church in New Canaan. Two days after his interview, on Memorial Day, the church called, inviting us back. We looked at the apartment and I was stunned. Thirteen rooms filled the top floor of a turn-of-the-century house with beautiful views of the church and its lush green lawns. Downstairs were staff offices, classrooms and meeting rooms, but most of the top floor was for the sexton's family. Bill was offered the job on the spot.

We moved in that summer and Bill started his work keeping the large physical plant running smoothly. Soon I was helping him. One day, as I was pushing a mop through the sanctuary, I picked up a bulletin a parishioner had dropped and stared at the Bible passage printed there. *These people believe God is working in their lives,* I thought with a start. I wondered if God was working in our lives too.

Across the hall from our apartment was the office of one of the ministers, the Reverend Maggie Minnick. She had short hair, a broad grin, and a booming laugh. Often I ran into her on the stairs. She always asked how I was feeling and how my pregnancy was going. Although I liked her, I kept my distance. My husband is an employee of the church, I told myself. We are not members.

What I couldn't tell anyone was that the pregnancy was not going well. At four months I went for my regular checkup, and the doctor told me my baby was too small. He determined that the baby wasn't due until Thanksgiving. *That can't be,* I thought. By my count the doctor was a month off. In September I started bleeding, and Bill took me to the emergency room, where an ultrasound revealed a rip in my placenta. The doctor seemed unconcerned. "Go home and keep your feet up for three days," he said. "You'll be fine." He also pointed out that my baby was too small to be due in another month. "You won't have this baby until Christmas."

"That's not possible," I said. He casually dismissed my fears. Back at St. Mark's, I paused outside Maggie's door. Then I reminded myself again: *We aren't part of the church. We just work in it.*

On October 26, at 6:00 AM, my water broke. Bill rushed me to the hospital. The fetal monitor indicated the baby was in distress, and I began to shake uncontrollably. I was wheeled into the delivery room, and after a difficult birth I heard someone murmur, "It's a boy."

I had to wait a long time to hear our baby cry. Everyone in the delivery room was somber. Someone held a bundle in front of me, but all I could see were two tiny nostrils before my son was whisked away. *What's wrong?*

A few hours later Bill took me to the newborn intensive care unit. Our baby was sleeping in an incubator. Although full term, he weighed only four pounds. He had big bulging eyes, still sealed shut. I put a latex-gloved hand through a porthole in the incubator and gently stroked his bony chest. Bill leaned against my shoulder as we stared through the transparent plastic.

Maggie, our first visitor, came to my room and said, "I've been to the ICU and prayed for the baby. I hope you don't mind."

For days no one could tell us what was wrong with our little boy, whom we'd named James. He wasn't sick. He didn't have lung trouble. He didn't need oxygen. But he was unable to suck and had to be fed formula through a tube in his nose. "He needs to gain weight," the doctor said. Physical therapists came in to help James, and after three weeks his eyes opened, but he lay there listless. Failure to thrive was the diagnosis.

I shuttled back and forth from the hospital to our top-floor apartment. Looking out the window to the auburn maples, brilliant in the golden sun, I prayed, truly prayed for maybe the first time. "God, don't let me be afraid," I asked. "And please help James."

After a month of intensive care, we took four-and-half-pound James home. He still had a feeding tube in his nose and was largely unresponsive to normal stimuli. The most frustrating thing was that doctors couldn't explain exactly what was wrong with him. The best they could come up with was that James was profoundly retarded, mentally and physically. "Expect very little improvement," we were told.

Struggling to get through one day of caring for him almost around the clock, I couldn't imagine what life would be like in the future. Would I be feeding him, clothing him, changing him for the rest of my days? To my amazement, though, I soon discovered I wasn't alone. Once when I had to take James to therapy, a woman from the church appeared on my doorstep, offering to babysit Catherine while I was gone. Not to worry, she said; she babysat children in the nursery. Another evening, a casserole was thrust into my arms.

"I hardly know these people," I told Maggie. "Why are they helping us?"

"That's the way we do things at St. Mark's," she said. "That's what a church is." Then she lifted James out of my arms and cuddled him. "God," she said, "thank you for the blessing of this wonderful boy. And give his parents fortitude." Her prayer gave me a sense of tranquility, something like the feeling I had on that night of my luminous visitors.

Maggie stopped by again and again. Just to have the companionship of another adult was a tremendous relief. When James was three months old, Maggie asked me if I'd consider enrolling him in something called STAR. "It's the Society to Advance the Retarded and Handicapped," said Maggie. "It meets right here at St. Mark's in one of our classrooms. It has its own staff of specialists. You'd have the opportunity to meet other parents whose kids have special needs."

Through the STAR parents' group Bill and I met an ear specialist who outfitted James with hearing aids, an eye doctor who prescribed special glasses, and an endocrinologist who taught me how to give growth-hormone injections at home. James learned to suck formula from a bottle. He reached for the mobile hanging above his crib. He turned his head toward the sound of my voice. He smiled at Bill.

One morning at STAR, while I was working with the physical therapist on a new exercise for James's legs, I noticed the director standing in the doorway with a tall, sandy-haired woman who looked about six months pregnant. For several minutes the woman watched James, gazing at him with sad eyes. After whispering to the director, she approached me and I answered her questions about James and his disabilities. Then she shook my hand and left the room.

By then I had become more involved in the church and started worshiping there. I took Catherine to Sunday school and James to the nursery. At Maggie's urging, we joined and later attended a three-day retreat with a group of other members. There, for the first time since James's birth, I had time to reflect on what we'd gone through.

At the close of the second night, I lingered in the chapel. Tears rolled down my cheeks as I talked to God. *Please show me Your presence in my life,* but even as I said the words I realized how God had been at work in our lives all along: the unexpected job at St. Mark's, the huge apartment, Maggie's friendship, the support of the church, and STAR. And again I recalled the luminous beings that had comforted me when I was pregnant. For the first time I understood who had sent them. "Do not be afraid," they had said, like so many of God's messengers.

A few months later I was picking James up at STAR when a tall, slender lady with sandy hair and a baby in her arms waved to get my attention. Almost immediately I recognized her.

"I've been looking for you," she said. "There's someone here I want you to meet." Carefully she pulled the blanket away from her sleeping baby's face. "When my husband and I learned that she had Down's syndrome, we made plans to give her up for adoption. I didn't think I could handle a handicapped child. But then I saw you and James that day. . . ." She couldn't finish the sentence.

"I know," I said, taking her hand. God sends His angels just when we need them and sometimes even before we know we need them.

The sweetest of all sounds is praise.
—XENOPHON

DAY BY DAY

ROBERTA L. MESSNER

Two o'clock in the morning—I woke up with nausea and a searing headache, as if a hammer were banging against my eye sockets and temples. My stomach convulsed. As I watched the luminous numbers on my bedside clock flip over, seemingly in slow motion, I asked myself how I could possibly bear the agony that was ahead. Minutes, hours, days of excruciating pain, the kind that reaches you even when you're asleep.

Pain had been a part of my life for twenty years, ever since I was diagnosed with neurofibromatosis in my early teens. This baffling disorder causes tumors to grow in my head, clinging to the long nerves under my skin, tenacious as leeches. Although benign, the tumors must be removed surgically or they can damage the nerves. But every time they're operated on, they come back again, larger and more painful than before.

Now I had thirty days before my next round of surgery, thirty days of trying to cope with the pain. Normally I could take medication for relief but not this time.

That very afternoon I had met with the surgeon who would perform the operation. "Roberta," he explained, "I know the pills you've been taking have aspirin in them. You'll have to stop using them until after the surgery. They create too much risk of hemorrhaging."

As a nurse, I understood and nodded. Inside I cringed. Even while taking this medication, the only effective one for me, I had days of agony. There were times when the short walk from the hospital parking lot to my office was like rolling a boulder up a mountain. Making my rounds, I pasted on a smile and counted the minutes until the medicine took hold, trying to concentrate on my patients' aches and pains instead of mine. While catching up on paperwork, I shut my office door, dimmed the lights, plugged my ears with Kleenex and wrote, holding an ice bag to my head. I kept a trash can by my desk for when I needed to vomit.

I can't possibly go that long without medication, I thought. I wouldn't be able to function. I would go mad from the pain. Now, at 2:00 AM, I was having my first glimpse of what it would be like. I staggered to the bathroom, doused a washcloth in cold water and held it to my eye, hoping to relieve the throbbing.

My whole life had been controlled by pain. The places I went, the career I chose, the friends I made. Once, just after I was diagnosed, I fainted in class while making a speech. *I will never take another class that requires public speaking,* I told myself. Anything to avoid the embarrassment.

The pain absorbed so much of my time and energy. It was isolating. I declined invitations to parties because I was afraid I'd feel too sick to go. I rarely formed friendships with people my own age because I feared they wouldn't understand my lack of energy or my having to change plans. I turned down professional opportunities. What if I couldn't handle the workload? What if the pain got too bad?

Still, nothing could be as bad as what I faced now. Thirty days without effective medication. Thirty days of unrelieved suffering. "Dear God," I spoke to the gloom, "what am I going to do now?"

Praise Him, came the answer. Praise Him? That was so contrary to my normal impulses, so contrary to my anger for being made to suffer, that I was shocked. How could I praise Him? Most of my prayer time was spent asking for help.

I went into the kitchen and got an ice pack out of the freezer. Sinking back on my bed, I held it against my face. In the darkness of the room, with the glow of the clock turning over the minutes as they passed, one by one, I thought again of the days ahead. The urge returned: Make it thirty days of praise. I closed my eyes. How would I do that?

An image of Harriet Love, my piano teacher, came to me. I had started taking lessons because I feared the tumors would take away my eyesight. Music would be one comfort left to me. I loved sitting next to Harriet at the piano bench, admiring the roses she picked from her garden. We began our Tuesday evening sessions with a prayer, then I put aside the pressures of work and the illness in order to concentrate on Bach, Clementi, or Chopin. For that one hour every week, my life was filled with light.

I flipped on my bedside lamp, grabbed a note card from the nightstand drawer and scribbled a few lines to her. "Thank you, Harriet, for our wonderful lessons and the time we have together in prayer. You are a godsend." The pain didn't go away, but for a little while I was able to get away from it and outside of myself. *I'll send her the note in the morning.*

Despite the sleepless night, I went to work with a renewed sense of purpose. "Praise Him," I told myself. Now I had a way to do that, focusing on the people God had brought into my life to ease its sorrows and strains.

Logging on to my computer, I found a memo from my coworker Barbara. Another person to be thankful for. I belonged to a computer prayer group she had started. I penned her my appreciation on another note card, then left it under the candy dish on her desk. When I ran into her in the hall she exclaimed, "You don't know what that note meant to me!" Funny, why had I never thanked her before?

The response was so satisfying that I looked for other people to thank as the days passed, and to each I wrote a note. My hairdresser had come up with a new hairstyle for me, bringing my bangs around my glasses, which disguised the bulges from the tumors. When I looked better, I felt better. And that's what I wrote her, praising God as I penned the letter.

I recalled all the help that my friend Jeanne had given me in nursing school. After classes I had gone to her house and played with her kids while she tutored me in chemistry. I hadn't seen her in years, but I wrote her a note. "Thanks for your friendship. Without you I never would have passed chemistry, let alone gotten an A on the final."

I started writing to people who were almost strangers. The piano salesman who found me a really good buy on a Steinway grand and took my old Kawai as a trade-in. Then there was the sympathetic optician. I was having problems getting lenses and frames that fit my face. One afternoon when I went to his shop, at my wit's end, he said reassuringly, "You're not going to leave here until we get this problem fixed." And we did.

Emboldened, I even took to writing several authors whose work I admired. Why would they want to hear from me? I thought. And then I reminded myself that thanking them was part of praising God. Their books and articles had brought so much pleasure to my life.

But as I expanded the circle of people I was grateful for, I stopped receiving responses to my letters. For instance, I wrote to my junior-high home economics teacher, Mrs. Barrett. What a wonder she was! Instead of forcing us to sew the same boring shifts, she allowed us to choose our own designs. "As long as I can hear those scissors crunch," she said. When I came up with the idea of having a fashion show, the class sewing dresses for the teachers, she embraced it wholeheartedly. "You made me feel like I could do anything," I wrote her, thanking God for Mrs. Barrett.

I waited and waited for an answer from her. All the while the pain continued. I sat at my desk with an ice pack, trash can nearby. At home, I lay on the family room sofa for hours, the blinds drawn, soothing music on the CD player, a sachet of fragrant herbs on my face. Of course, I knew it was unreasonable of me to expect an immediate response. Then I realized: That's not why I was writing. The prayers and praise were enough. It was the act of praying, not the outcome, that was helping.

By the time Mrs. Barrett contacted me, the praise therapy had made a permanent difference in my outlook. Instead of dwelling on my pain, letting it isolate me, the notes I wrote showed me the connections I had with so many people, from my hairdresser to the checkout man at Convenient Food Mart.

I discovered I could praise God silently through the normal routine of a day. I printed the names of people I was grateful for on yellow Post-it notes and stuck them all over: next to the computer screen, on the dashboard, on the refrigerator. When I felt the familiar throbbing in my head, I concentrated on one of the names and said a prayer. At work, during a meeting that seemed interminable, I mentally went around the table and looked for one thing in each person I was thankful for and prayed. Concentrated praying. Although I was battling a disease that was beyond my power to change, I felt less of a victim. My life belonged to me again.

Yes, there were moments when praise took a back burner to doubt and my pain seemed unendurable. But always I returned to thanksgiving, to prayer. In the end, the pain, the very thing that had threatened to separate me from God, brought me closer to Him.

Thirty days went quickly. My surgery was successful, and afterward I went back on my medication. By then I'd found another treatment that works, a spiritual one. Pain will always be with me; so will God. He is more powerful than any suffering; and when I praise Him, I feel His love drawing me near, closer to Him than to anything else, even pain.

TITLE INDEX

AUTHOR INDEX

ACKNOWLEDGMENTS

ALLEN, WALTER. "Sailing Steerage to New York" from *All in a Lifetime*, 1959. Reprinted by permission of Harold A. Ober Associates, Inc. FORSTER, E. M. "From Notes on English Character" from *Abinger Harvest*. Copyright © 1936, renewed 1964 by Edward Morgan Forster. Reprinted by permission of Harcourt, Inc. FROMM, ERICH. "The Love Underlying Friendship" from *The Art of Loving*. Copyright © 1956 by Erich Fromm, renewed 1984 by Annis Fromm. Reprinted by permission of HarperCollins Publishers, Inc. GIBRAN, KAHLIL. "It Is When You Give of Yourself" from *The Prophet* by Kahlil Gibran, copyright © 1923 by Kahlil Gibran and renewed 1951 by Administrators C.T.A. of Kahlil Gibran Estate and Mary G. Gibran. Used by permission of Alfred A. Knopf, a division of Random House, Inc and The Gibran National Committee. HECHT, BEN. "My Hundred Friends" from *A Child of the Century*. Copyright © 1954 by Ben Hecht. Published by Simon & Schuster. KENNEDY, PAMELA. "Long-Distance Friends," "Look Again," "A Blessed Friendship," and "Faithful Friends." Used by permission of Pamela Kennedy. LEWIS, C. S. "A Common Quest" from *The Quotable Lewis*. Copyright © 1989 by Wayne Martindale and Jerry Root, editors. Used by permission of Tyndale House Publishers, Inc. RAMELKAMP, BETSY. "The Tamale-maker's Gift of Friendship" from *Christian Science Monitor*, Vol. 88, April 16, 1996. Used by permission of the author. REPPLIER, AGNES. "A Small Tragedy" from *Eight Decades*. Copyright © 1937. Published by Houghton Mifflin Co. ROONEY, ANDREW A. "Wally" from *Pieces of My Mind* by Andrew A. Rooney. Copyright © 1984 by Essay Productions, Inc. Used by permission of Scribner, an imprint of Simon & Schuster Adult Publishing Group. TABER, GLADYS. "A Countrywoman's Journal" from *Stillmeadow Calendar: A Countrywoman's Journal* Copyright © 1967 by Gladys Taber. Published by J. B. Lippincott Company. WALWORTH, DOROTHY. "A Woman to Warm Your Heart By" from *The Baltimore Sun*, March 5, 1944, and condensed by *Reader's Digest*, April 1944. WILDER, LAURA INGALLS. "A Constant Friend" taken from *Little House in the Ozarks* by Laura Ingalls Wilder. Edited by Stephen W. Hines (Nashville: Thomas Nelson, 1991). Used by permission of Stephen W. Hines. Our sincere thanks to the following author whom we were unable to locate: Harry B. Hawes for "Concerning Friendship."

All other stories are reprinted from *Guideposts Magazine*. Copyright © Guideposts, Carmel, NY 10512.

All possible care has been taken to fully acknowledge the ownership and use of every selection in this book. If any mistakes or omissions have occurred, they will be corrected in subsequent editions, provided notification is sent to the publisher.